Boxer's Start-Up:

A Beginner's
Guide to Boxing

Text and Photography
By Doug Werner

Start-Up Sports **#9**

Tracks Publishing
San Diego, California

Boxer's Start-Up:
A Beginner's Guide to Boxing
By Doug Werner

Start-Up Sports / Tracks Publishing
140 Brightwood Avenue
Chula Vista, CA 91910
619-476-7125 Fax 619-476-8173

Publisher's Cataloging in Publication

Werner, Doug.
    Boxer's start-up : a beginner's guide to boxing / by Doug Werner.

    p. cm. – (Start-up sports ; #9)
Includes bibliographical references and index.
Preassigned LCCN: 98-60534.
ISBN: 1-884654-09-6.

    1. Boxing.   I. Title.   II. Series.

GV1133.W47 1998   796.83
                             QBI98-499

To Alan Lachica

Acknowledgements:

Alison Thatcher

Lance Goldman

Katrina Gaede

Teri Youngs

Jordan Ressler

Ryan Broomburg

Jonathan Gruber

Kathleen Wheeler

Red Werner

Ann Werner

Phyllis Carter

Jim Clinkscales

Mark Suchomel

Lynn's Photo

ColorType

North Shores Printery

Doug Ward

Shilpa Bakre

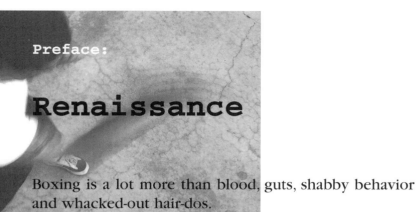

Renaissance

Boxing is a lot more than blood, guts, shabby behavior and whacked-out hair-dos.

Underneath boxing's ugly public perception lies the pursuit of complete physical conditioning, athletic grace and essential self-defense for both men and women. *Boxer's Start-Up: A Beginner's Guide to Boxing* explores boxing as a confidence building and practical method of defending oneself, as well as a fun, sure-fire way to get into the best shape of your life. Included is information about equipment, safety, the boxer's workout, offensive and defensive skills and history.

I believe that there is a new market for a new boxing book. Mainstream interest in boxing and the boxer's workout is higher than it has been in 20 years.

First and foremost, the fitness movement has become enamored with the boxer's workout. The drills are aerobically supercharged, improve balance and coordination and teach basic self-defense for both sexes. Public awareness of the benefits of the boxer's workout has cast a brighter light on the sport in general.

Second, the new champions are definitely a cut above the thugs and grandstanders of years past and will most certainly convert legions of new fans. There's no doubt that Evander Holyfield projects a better image than Mike Tyson. Young up-and-comers, like the clean-cut and clean-living welterweight champion Oscar De La Hoya, promise to usher in a new era of respectability as well as a new crop of female fans. And of course, George Foreman single handedly forced a nation of middle-aged Americans to take another look at boxing (and their midsections) during the '90s with his courageous comeback and heavyweight sense of humor.

Third, media coverage is at an all-time high. HBO, ESPN and Pay-Per-View each regularly broadcast boxing matches and report record ratings for 1997.

Finally, the advent of women's boxing over the last five years has broken down the men's club door, changing forever the sport's appeal and horizons. The most exciting bout during the evening of the Tyson-Bruno mismatch of 1997 was the undercard that featured female boxing's top competitor Christy Martin. She has also been featured on the cover of *Sports Illustrated*.

My reasons for writing this book also include a more traditional point of view. My gut take is that most every guy (and maybe every person) desires the self-confidence that comes from knowing how to defend oneself. Boxing is still the grandaddy of self-defense, and despite martial arty trends, is still the heart and soul of American contact sport.

Doug Werner
Tracks Publishing / Start-Up Sports

Contents

Women in boxing:
Changing the sport forever.

Good News

PRIMAL

So I got this idea to take up boxing. Nothing in particular nurtured the idea, it just dawdled in my noggin (as such thoughts do) and stayed there. It's my belief that if something sticks around in my head for any length of time, it's meant to be dealt with no matter what or why.

Thinking about it, though, I can come up with some pretty good reasons. Boxing is at the heart of physical toughness. It's the barest art of self-defense. It can be the rawest measure of a person. It's the most basic of competitions where fears are met and overcome or all is lost. It's the ideal vehicle for unfettered aggression. Short of actual hand-to-hand combat, it's the ultimate contest between two people.

It's primal. Like sex, making money and laughing. All guys (way down deep) wanna be desirable love machines, happily rolling in green and capable of stopping anyone at anytime with a lethal right hand.

MEGA WORKOUT

The boxer's workout will get you into the best shape of your life. I've been involved with several sports over the

years and not one of them comes close to the type of physical conditioning that boxing demands. The boxer's workout improves everything: strength, endurance, coordination, you name it. An hour of bag beating, sparring and skipping rope will leave you soaked, spent and exhilarated. Three months of this regime will shape you up, put a bounce in your step and instill a special kind of self assurance that the TV gym gizmologists can only dream of.

ATHLETIC GRACE

Hey, it's boxing bay-be. Exercise drills are structured around three-minute rounds of aerobically supercharged effort designed to forge you into a better athlete. No less. You'll sweat and burn, sure. But you'll also become a better balanced, more coordinated, sharper reflexed, longer lasting human being. Try getting that out of a stairmaster.

CRANIAL RELIEF

What it does for your head is remarkable.

This ain't news: Day-to-day life can be one ultimately meaningless, yet immediately urgent and oh-so-annoying snafu, obligation or requirement after another. Fear and rage zoom in and out of our minds like bats from hell whether we're fighting to put food in our mouths or simply trying to deal with traffic. But after 20 minutes on the heavy bag it's all gone. Beat the bag and you'll beat the blues, brother. No lie.

THE ULTIMATE ATTITUDE ADJUSTMENT

And rediscover self-assurance (remember that?). Boxing is the great and grand art of defending yourself with your hands. Knowing how it's done will change the way

you walk into a room, stroll down the street or meet someone new. It's not a bully thing at all. It's probably one of the oldest and purest forms of confidence a person can have.

CONFIDENCE <u>NOT</u> TO FIGHT

More on this confidence stuff. Acquiring boxing skills won't make you any more likely to get into physical confrontations outside the gym. Actually, the desire to settle things violently will become weaker — because you have nothing to prove, you won't be compelled to prove it. It's a martial arts type of thought and it applies to boxing as well. When you are truly confident in your ability to defend yourself, the minor confrontations in your life stay minor. Especially in your mind.

WHOOPIE!

And it's fun. The three minutes of each round is insanely intense and exciting. It's like being in the greatest action movie ever made. Heck, I get giddy.

SWEAT! VIOLENCE! FEAR! (OH MY!)

Yeah it's a alotta work, but what isn't? Don't be afraid of the sweat and strain. You'll learn to glory in it. Don't be put off by the violence of the effort. It's the sweetest release. Don't be afraid of trading punches. With the proper gear and supervision, boxing is not a dangerous slugfest, but a remarkably refined exercise in athletic grace and technique. Besides, facing your fears in the ring (or anywhere else) is freedom. Believe it.

INSTRUCTION

This book will detail certain aspects of the boxer's workout including some boxing technique and specific drills. This will be more than enough to get you acquainted with the sport in general and to get you started with a great fitness program.

However, if you're going to get into sparring, it's recommended that you hook up with an accredited coach and an accredited boxing program. If you're gonna throw punches you want to be trained and supervised by those who know. That's how you'll learn safely and properly. Without proper supervision, you and your neighbor will just be rumbling around with bloody noses. Or worse.

In the United States the umbrella boxing organization for amateur or Olympic-style boxing is the United States Amateur Boxing, Inc. or USA Boxing. They sponsor a host of programs from developing the sport and its athletes at the local, regional and national levels, to sponsoring national and international dual competitions and selecting teams for international events, including the Olympic Games, World Championships and Pan American Games. USA Boxing has programs all over the country and to contact one near you, call or write:

USA Boxing
719-578-4506
Fax: 719-632-3426
E-mail: usaboxing@aol.com

The differences between Olympic-style and professional boxing are very important and are explored more fully later in the book.

DEMARCATING THE DANGER ZONE
The label on my headgear reads:

> **WARNING: Users of this product are subject to personal injury. Severe head, neck, and other injuries including death and paralysis may occur despite using this equipment.**

Are you still there?

First of all, if it's just the workout you're after, there's no contact and therefore no punching in your face. The workout involves contests between you and a skip rope, a heavy bag or someone wearing punch mitts.

Sparring is another matter but still a stage of intensity below amateur competition. Sparring is a closely supervised bout between individuals who are, by and large, trying to fine tune their technique. Proper headgear, mouthpiece, wraps, sparring gloves and groin protection are always worn.

Sparring is really a boxing *lesson* — the boxers are the students and the referee is an accredited coach. Or one of the boxers is an accredited coach. It's not about winning or beating someone up. It's about developing your own form and style — working out the kinks in your own game. It's not so much a contest between you and the other guy as it is a measure of your own boxing skills.

The scope of this book is the boxer's workout and a little sparring as defined above. The intent here is to spread the good word about boxing's benefits to mind, body and soul.

Inflicting or receiving injury is not the message.

If you spar with the proper protective gear, under properly supervised conditions and with a healthy attitude, your chances of avoiding major mishaps are probably pretty good.

However, it's important to emphasize the fact that we are talking about boxing. Punches are thrown and leather is eaten. If you spar you're gonna get tagged on occasion and hurties happen. They just do.

If you don't wanna get hit, don't spar. Stick with the boxer's workout.

Chapter One:

Learning ... to box
ain't no overnight thing

Your introduction to boxing is a building process that will take awhile. This sport incorporates a complex array of skills that develop and dovetail through training and repeated effort. You'll think through them at first, then muscle memory takes over as you put in the hours.

As you train you'll condition your body to function at the high levels required to successfully last a succession of three-minute rounds with a teeny-tiny one-minute break in between. It doesn't sound like much but it'll be one of the hardest things you'll ever do. The three-minute round, by the way, is based on the actual time of a round in competition. Likewise the one-minute break.

Don't even think about sparring for a few months. Without knowing the skills, you'll box like Doris Day.

And without conditioning, you won't last a minute before you become a wheezing wreck.

Training is everything. Respect it.

And for heaven's sake, have fun with it. Stick with it and you'll never regret the hard work. Figure around six months of training to acquire some basic boxing skills and the proper conditioning to successfully spar three three-minute rounds. Figure a whole lot more to get better.

Watching Fights

After a few lessons you can watch competitive bouts with more understanding and interest. Furthermore, they serve as a great learning tool. After all, you're watching the guys that have, more or less, put it all together.

Chapter Two:

Boxing Gear

SHOPPING LISTS

**A List: Right away
for the boxer's workout:**
T-shirts
Shorts or sweats
Athletic socks
Athletic footwear
Wraps
Bag gloves
Heavy bag
Jump rope
Punch mitts
(if you have a partner)

**B List: Later on
for sparring:**
Headgear
Mouthguard
Sparring gloves
Groin protector

This is the stuff you gotta have. You'll look at the loaded catalogs and see all kinds of other things, but this is all you really need to develop some basic skills over a six-month period. In fact, you shouldn't have to worry about anything on the B List until your initial training (which could very well last six months) is finished.

You're not going to spar with anyone until you've mastered your basic skills and can comfortably last three or four active three-minute rounds on the heavy bag. That's the right way to do it. That's the safe and sane way to develop as a boxer. Period.

Going over the lists in detail.

A List:

Assuming you already know what T-shirts, shorts and athletic socks are, we'll start with the footwear.

Athletic Footwear: Sneakers that fit well are fine for now. Don't bother with actual boxing shoes. If you're training in a gym you may need to avoid dark soles that could mark up the floor. High tops are nice because of the extra support.

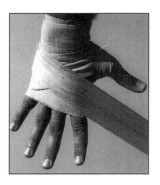

Wraps: Before you put on gloves you must wrap your hands for support and protection with long strips of cloth called wraps. Get the kind that have Velcro ties since they're the most convenient to use. I like the Mexican-style wraps because they're longer and provide better protection. $6.

Bag Gloves: Bag gloves are different from sparring or competition gloves. Bag gloves have just enough padding to protect a boxer's hands as he whales on the heavy bag. Training or sparring gloves are more carefully designed to protect the hands and offset the force of a blow from a sparring partner.

Bag gloves come in various weights, styles and degrees of quality and convenience. For my training, I purchased a quality pair of 12-ounce leather gloves with a wide Velcro strap closure for easy on and off. These are about the best money can buy, and depending on your size, cost $50 or $60 in 1998 dollars. The cheapest pair costs half as much, but heck, for $25 more you can get professional durability, design and safety. They're your hands, it's your choice. Like a good pair of shoes, make sure they fit and stay secure on your paws.

Heavy Bag: You're gonna need something to punch. Heavy bags come in a variety of styles, but your basic bag is about 14 inches in diameter, 42 inches high and weighs 70 pounds. I got a canvas bag with a so called regular or hard fill versus a soft fill. The soft fill simply has a thicker foam liner. Mine came with hanging chains, hooks and a swivel so it could be hung from a beam (or as in my case from a rope slung over the roof and tied off to a tree in my backyard — whatever works!). I spent about $80 for it.

Jump Rope: Should be one of your cheapest purchases. Under $10.

Punch Mitts: These are pads which slip over the hands in order to target and catch punches. If you have a workout buddy, one of you can practice stuff while the other makes like a punching bag. They are very effective tools if utilized properly. A good pair runs around $50.

B List:
Only if you wish to spar, and only when you're ready.

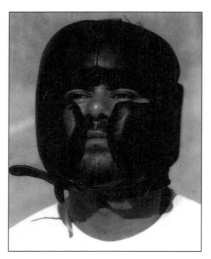

Headgear: Don't skimp here! Purchase a design that covers as much as possible: chin, cheeks and forehead. There are models with a face bar that protects the nose and mouth, but breathing in them is a little difficult. My headgear has lace straps that really keep the thing tight on my head. This is very important. You don't want your headgear slipping over your eyes after every punch you take. I spent $70 on mine.

Mouthguard: Very important unless you plan on never getting hit. The "boil and bite" variety are inexpensive (under $10) and work fine. "Boil and bite" refers to the method used to form-fit this type of guard to your teeth. First it's boiled in water to make it pliable, then you place it in your mouth, press it with fingers to your teeth and bite down. The mouthpiece is made of material that doesn't retain heat and won't burn you.

Sparring Gloves: As stated previously, sparring gloves are designed differently from bag gloves since they'll be used to strike a person and not a bag. My gloves are 14 ounces, padded with two inches of multi-layered foam and are secured with large Velcro straps for easy on and off. I paid $135 for a very good pair of leather gloves. Don't skimp here either.

Groin Protector: The mother of all jock straps. This is a girdle-type thing that protects groin, hips and kidneys. I spent $45 on mine. It's bright red and you can see me coming a mile away. By the way, a simple jock and cup aren't quite enough protection in this sport.

Note for Female Boxers
Women have their own designs to choose from for groin and breast protection. Gloves are specifically manufactured for women, as well.

Where to Buy

Your local sporting goods store or outlet will have stuff, but I suggest you buy from a catalog (often the gear found in the large retail outlets is crap).

Everlast: 718-993-0100
Ringside: 913-888-1719
Title Boxing: 913-831-1122

Geared up to spar. Quality headgear, training gloves and groin protector provide safety and protection. The groin protector can be worn over or under shorts.

Please note that although full protection isn't worn by the boxers in all the photos in this book, this in no way condones sparring without wearing proper protection as recommended above. If boxer's aren't completely suited up they are demonstrating technique only and not actually sparring. In most cases specific points of technique were better presented without gearing up because equipment tended to obscure details. DW

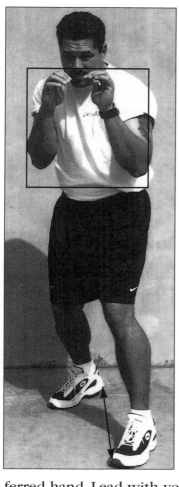

Chapter Three:

Boxer's Stance & Basic Footwork

The foundation upon which all boxing skills are based is the stance. (Color me slow, but it took 15 lesson hours for mine to fall into place.)

Boxer's Stance: Basic Position, Legs & Feet

In front of an imaginary opponent, position yourself sideways so that you present a shoulder to your target. By and large, your leading side is the opposite of your preferred hand. Lead with your left shoulder if you're right-handed and vise versa. Your feet should be about shoulder width apart.

If you're leading with the left shoulder, place your right foot out in front of yourself so that the heel of your right foot lines up with the toe of your left.

With both heels in place, swivel your feet 45 degrees

toward your target. Flex your knees and bend a bit at the hips keeping your back fairly straight. Slightly lift your back heel off the deck.

This is more or less a basic athletic posture in which you're balanced and solid on your feet. A push from any direction will not cause you to easily stumble. You are ready to move in any direction the action dictates. This is the lower half of the "on guard" or ready position.

Boxer's Stance: Arms, Hands & Head

To complete the northern half, tuck your elbows in close to your sides and raise your forearms up straight. Arrange the pillars of your arms so they protect that area of your torso that faces the target. Hold your arms with just enough tension to keep them upright. This

position shouldn't be tight or rigid. Bend your head forward so that you're viewing your opponent partially through your eyebrows. At this point, your hands should be about chin to cheek level. Palms are turned in.

There you go. This is your boxer's stance. You are equally prepared to throw punches as well as defend against them. In this ready position you are relaxed. Never tense.

Box Trot

Boxing is a lot more like dancing than you might imagine. One immediately thinks of using hands and arms when you bout but not so much legs and feet. However, being able to move rapidly and economically, balanced and ready to attack or defend, is vital.

Moving Forward: The lead or left foot steps first then the right foot closes the distance. Steps are small. Note that the stance remains intact throughout. When moving back, the back or right foot leads.

Moving to the Side: Left leads going left and right leads going right. Steps stay low to the deck.

The idea in all movement is to maintain the integrity of your boxer's stance. Basically, that means you never over step, cross over or bring your feet together.

There are four directions you may go: toward your opponent, back from your opponent, to the side you are mostly facing and to the side at your back.

In each direction you have a lead foot which initiates the movement and opens your stance. After the lead foot has taken a step, close the distance with your trailing foot and regain a shoulder width stance. Steps are short in length and taken close to the surface of the floor — almost in a slide.

Pivot & Slide

Quick changes in direction are made by sweeping the rear foot in either direction and pivoting off the ball of your lead foot. Again, the sweeping motion of the foot is held close to the floor surface.

Pivoting: The front foot acts as a hub for the rear foot as it swings around. Again, in no way does the movement upset the balance and stability of the boxer's stance.

SNAP! those punches

Chapter Four:

Basic Punches

Make a Fist

You'll probably get it right the first time you try except for one thing. For the record, the thumb rests below the tucked in fingers, not curled inside, but then you knew that. What you might not know is that the fist is not clenched until just before point of impact. Hands are held loose in readiness (like everything else) — even on the way to the  target. Ideally the fist tightens as it lands and immediately relaxes as it's pulled back. You don't use energy until you need it. And that's a law that underlines everything you do in boxing.

Note for Southpaws

For convenience, most of the book will focus on instruction for right-handed or left-foot-forward readers. If you're left-handed or prefer to box with the right foot forward, reverse the instructions where applicable.

Jab

Meet the most important punch in boxing — the one you'll use the most in your boxing career, whether you're fighting for fitness or glory.

The jab doesn't compromise a boxer's defensive posture. Chin remains tucked behind the left shoulder and feet remain poised in the guard position.

The jab is a quick offensive strike.

In the boxer's stance your fists are held in a relaxed, palms-in, ready position. The jab is a punch thrown with the leading hand straight from the chin in a direct line toward your target. As the hand leaves its guard position next to your chin, the fist rotates a quarter to a half notch. As the punch is delivered, the fist gradually clenches and is completely clenched just before impact. It is then immediately relaxed and withdrawn into the guard position.

The jab is the busiest weapon in boxing because it can be thrown quickly without compromising a boxer's defensive posture. It's utilized to score, to keep opponents at bay, to set up combinations and power punches and to wear down defenses.

Although the jab is not considered a power punch, an effective use of the jab over the course of a bout will cause a considerable deal of damage. A boxer can also learn to stiffen his jab by turning his hips with the punch and stepping into its delivery.

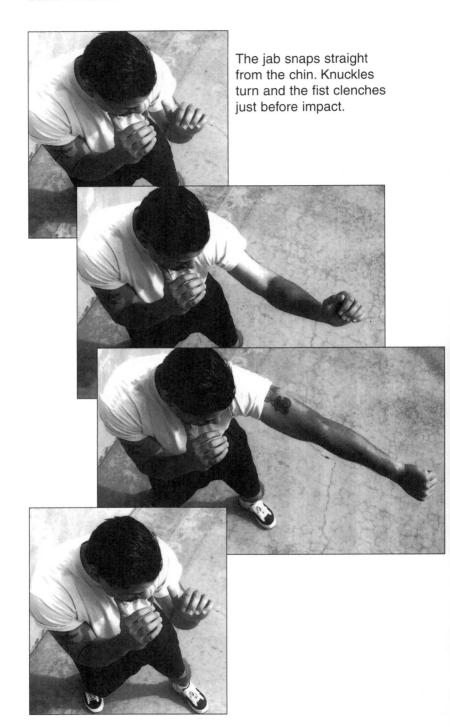

The jab snaps straight from the chin. Knuckles turn and the fist clenches just before impact.

The jab is an arm punch and doesn't affect the integrity of the guard position. Balance and mobility are maintained throughout.

I'm told that the jab is the only punch to use in a street fight as it can be thrown with a great deal of effectiveness without risking exposure, loss of balance or mobility. The wallop of a crisply thrown jab is more than enough to break a nose and hopefully end the dispute.

Watch any competitive bout and the jab count far exceeds that of any other punch. It's the bread and butter of offensive boxing.

Breathing
Exhale as you deliver all your punches in short, spitting wheezes. Believe it or not, the tendency is to hold your breath when punching. Perhaps it's the excitement, but at any rate, not breathing is a bad habit to get into.

Jab Notes
The jab is thrown directly from the chin with no wind-up or shrugging of the shoulders. The jab snaps toward its target and is pulled back immediately. A quick recovery is just as important as a quick delivery.

The straight right is one of the most powerful weapons in boxing. It is thrown off the right leg with torquing hips and torso. After the punch lands it's imperative that you recover to guard position immediately.

The right is initiated by a weight transfer to the right side and a pivoting right foot.

Straight Right

Your first favorite punch will be the one you throw with your preferred hand — naturally!

For the right-handed boxer, it's the straight right. From the guard position, the right hand is thrown straight from the chin on a direct line to the target. Unlike the jab, which is an arm-powered punch, the right is powered by a torquing torso and a pivoting right foot. Feel your back get into this one. The punch should accelerate and explode as the right heel of your pivoting foot swings outward. After impact the hand is sharply returned to guard.

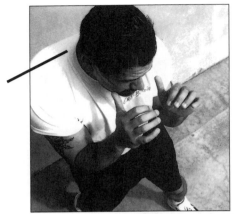

The back definitely gets behind a right. Note the ninety degree sweep of the shoulders.

Because of the weight transfer involved, the straight right is considered a power punch. But the weight transfer is also the weakness of power punches because for a nano-second the boxer is without a balanced boxer's stance, and is therefore somewhat exposed. Hence the importance of high tailing it back to guard. The risk of throwing this punch too often far outweighs the natural pleasure of launching your favorite hand. The straight right is best utilized behind the jab or as a counter after a defensive move.

Right Notes

The straight right should be thrown straight from the chin without wind-up or dips of the shoulder. The punch accelerates as it tracks toward the target. Immediately before the explosion the fist clenches. Tension is immediately released as the hand snaps back to guard.

Straight punches are thrown directly from chin to target without a dip or lifting the elbow.

Left Hook

The legendary left hook is the most difficult punch to learn. Unlike the jab and straight right, the left hook has mysterious nuances that simply take time for most boxers to discover and assimilate.

The hook is generally misunderstood. Most beginners think the left hook is some sort of sweeping, round-house punch thrown and powered by a loopy left arm. I did, anyway. But it isn't anything like that.

The hook is an inside power punch. It's most effective when you're close to your opponent. The punch begins with a weight transfer to your left side. From the guard position the left elbow is brought up, almost parallel to the floor, so that the arm forms a sort of hook (hence the name). At the same time the fist is rotated either palm down for a very close target or palm-in for targets farther away.

Here's the secret. The arm is held in place as described above, and the punch is delivered by pivoting left foot, left leg and torso sharply to the right in a powerful, one-piece torquing action. The arm doesn't move independently of the whole. Like a gate swinging around its hinged post, this punch is powered by leg, hips, back and everything else in the barn. When it's thrown properly, it's one of the mighty weapons in boxing and is held in very high esteem.

When I work the hook, my coach tells me to *crush peanuts* with the ball of my left foot as I swing it around and to think *hey buddy, come on over here!* as I bring the punch to completion by tucking it into my chest

The power of the hook comes from arm, leg, hips and torso swinging around a pivoting left foot.

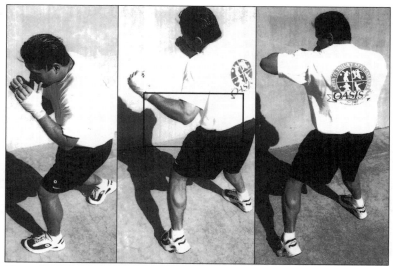

Note that the left elbow travels in the same plane as the hips. The left arm doesn't fly out or deliver itself independent of the whole.

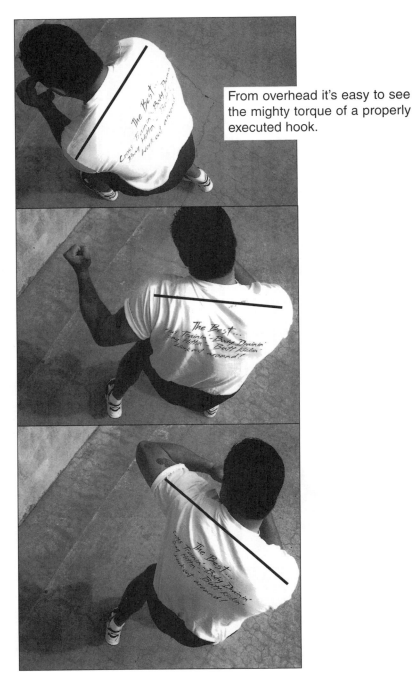

From overhead it's easy to see the mighty torque of a properly executed hook.

(like I'm hugging him high around the neck). Like all punches, the hook accelerates as it tracks to the target, the fist clenches before impact and is sharply returned to the guard position along with everything else that went for the ride.

Remember, recovery is everything. Punches should never hang. Punches SNAP! Think acceleration, SNAP!, recovery.

| Load up | Accelerate | **SNAP!** |

Left Uppercut

Uppercuts are stock and staple for inside fighting and are thrown with power coming from the legs and torso. They are not wind-up arm punches. From the guard position, dip the left shoulder so that your elbow nears your hip. At the same time rotate the fist palm-up. Without cocking the arm back or winding-up, propel this punch with the left side of your body. Accelerate, SNAP! and recover. The right uppercut is a mirror image of the left.

Punch Reminders

All punching action is best executed from a balanced boxer's stance. This ensures power, accuracy and recovery. Punching off balance is ineffective and risks maximum exposure.

Jabs and straight rights or lefts are delivered directly from the chin with no preamble (wind-up, dips, shrugs).

All punches are SNAPPED! Accelerate, SNAP! and recover. This includes sharp delivery and sharp recovery. A punch that hangs or is not recovered immediately exposes an entire half of a boxer to attack.

Guard Up!

Never forget the hand that isn't punching. While one hand is attacking the other is in guard position. This is especially crucial (yet easy to forget!) when both hands are busy executing combinations of punches.

The left uppercut begins with a dip and weight transfer to the left side. The elbow doesn't draw back before it's launched. Instead, the power comes from an upward thrust of the legs and hips.

The classic one-two combination starts with a jab followed by a weight transfer to the right side.

Immediately throw a straight right and recover. The action is crisp, quick and flowing – BOOM! BOOM!

Chapter Five:

Basic Combinations

A solid boxing offense includes an array of punches that can be effectively thrown in combination with one another. In other words, two or more punches properly delivered in a given attack are usually better than one.

Double and Triple Jabs
These are simply jabs thrown one after the other. Care must be taken to recover properly after each one in order to maximize power. This is an effective way to deliver a bunch of punches safely from a distance.

One-Two
That's right. This is the original one-two punch combo of sport literary and celluloid fame. The combination includes a jab followed by a straight right. The classic goal is to land a clean jab at the head that lifts the chin so that you can rock it with a hard right hand.

The left jab is thrown as described (SNAP!), recovered to guard, then the straight right is immediately launched (SNAP!) and recovered to guard. Throughout the action and after, you should feel solid over your feet. Otherwise, you're probably reaching or not recovering properly.

One-Two-Three

Add to the left jab and straight right combination the left hook. This is a very natural flow of punches as the weight shifts from one foot to the other. After the jab and straight right, your weight is over the left foot creating the perfect opportunity to unload the left hook. The classic goal here is to expose the chin with the jab, tag the chin with the right and clobber the guy on the temple with the left. One, two, three — outta there!

Right-Left-Right
Left-Right-Left

These are power punch combinations utilizing the straight right and the left hook. The challenge is to coordinate the weight shifts in order to properly execute each of these torso twisting bombshells. As one punch lands, you should be weighted perfectly to throw the next one.

It's easy to turn these into arm punches when you throw them in flurries, but without the body behind them they aren't as effective. It's also difficult to maintain proper form, especially with the hook. These combinations are among an in-fighter's favorite weapons because the attack flies from two angles.

Return to Guard

It's important to remember that after every punch the hand must return to guard. It's easy to forget in all the flailing, but without full recovery, half of your head is exposed and punches aren't so powerful. The tendency to drop hands is directly correlated to fatigue. It's the first thing to go.

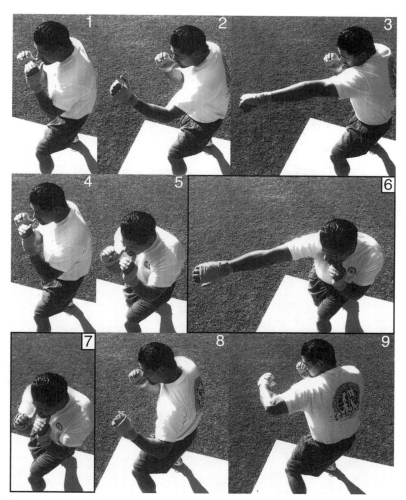

The one-two-three combination includes jab, straight right and left hook. There's harmony among these punches due largely to the shift of weight from right to left during the execution of the right. In other words, the right naturally sets up the left.

Combinations that include straight punches, hooks and uppercuts are particularly effective because the attack comes from various angles. Note that sides are traded with each punch (left, right, left, right and so on). There is a natural flow from side to side that enhances the delivery of each punch.

Combinations Including Uppercuts

Combining jabs, straight rights and left hooks with uppercuts is a dizzying feat, and absolutely devastating to an opponent because stuff is coming in from all directions. It's difficult to master the flow from one punch to the other and to execute them fully and properly. It's difficult enough to master the transitions from jab to straight right to hook ... heck it's hard enough just to learn the hook.

But practicing these flurries is a great coordination drill. A good six-punch drill includes a jab, a straight right, a left uppercut, a straight right, a left hook and finally a right uppercut.

Shadowboxing

After learning the basic footwork and punches, you can begin to practice one of the oldest and cheapest training methods there is: shadowboxing. All you really need is you, but it's a tremendous boost to box in front of a reflecting surface.

Shadowboxing is a great way to study and perfect your form and should never be underestimated. It's the one time your eyes are focused on your reflection instead of on a punching target. This is when you practice the entire boogie-woogie: footwork, rhythm, punches and defenses. You can drill these elements individually as well as a whole symphony of moving parts. Outside of viewing yourself on video (not a bad idea!) it's the only way you can see how you really look.

In your boxer's stance, practice moving in all four directions: up, back, frontside and backside. Next, incorporate some jabs with your steps. Stepping up or stepping backside, throw *as* you step with your left foot. Stepping back or frontside, throw *after* you've stepped and set your left foot.

Long rhythm is a mellow back and forth rocking from front to back. Feet remain planted. Note the head moves a head-width with each rock.

Boxer's Rhythm

Let's really mix it up. Boxers never really stand completely still. There should always be some sort of motion going on between steps and punches to keep you primed, pumped and ready for action.

There's the long rhythm, which is a kind of a mellow back-and-forth bouncing between the feet, and there's the short rhythm, which is a more aggressive side-to-side thing that involves moving the head and shoulders.

One of the all-time rivalries in boxing history showcased the two rhythm styles: Muhammad Ali and Joe Frazer.

Short rhythm is a brisk side-to-side movement. Again, the feet remain planted and the head moves a head-width with each rock. Rhythm is suspended when a boxer steps or pivots.

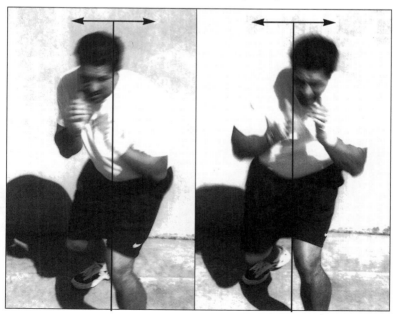

Muhammad Ali was the classic long-rhythm guy. His game was outside fighting -- using the jab and moving around the outskirts of an opponent's range. His arch rival, Joe Frazer, was an inside fighter and the classic short-rhythm boxer. Since inside fighters are always within the striking zone of an opponent, Frazer had to keep the noggin bobbin' at a brisk pace in order to make himself a harder target to hit.

Practice the two rhythms until they become natural and fluid -- like dancing -- and incorporate them into your shadowboxing routine. Remember, you don't boogie when you step or throw punches.

Getting it together in front of the mirror may take some time. Developing an inner beat is a personal thing, and combined with the stepping and punching, gets a little tricky. But keep at it. Good form goes hand in hand with technical proficiency. Getting it right will enhance your skills and looking sharp builds self-confidence.

Chapter Six:

Application: Whaling on the Heavy Bag

Shadowboxing is great training, but hammering on the heavy bag is all that and more. It's a mighty workout, terrific for sharpening and strengthening punches and a wonderful release of tension. It may sound bland — whaling away at a load suspended from the ceiling for minutes on end — but it's actually alotta fun and (dare I say this in a boxing book?) therapeutic.

No matter what's ailing you upstairs, three good rounds on the bag will rest the twisting knot in your mind and guarantee a better night's sleep.

Hanging the Bag
Keep in mind when you suspend the bag that it needs to be secured to something very strong. Your bag weighs 70 pounds and you're gonna be pounding the hell out of it. It'll be swinging, unless you secure the bottom

somehow, so you'll need room for the sway as well as room to move around it. Mine is suspended outside over the patio from an overhanging roof where the violent thrashing, grunts and flying sweat is of no great bother. But then I live in San Diego, California. If you must go inside, keep in mind that working the bag is very loud (it sounds like war) and soggy. Your wife, and especially your dogs, will not want the thing in the living room.

It's a good idea to have some help when you put the thing up and take it down. It's heavy and you'll be using a ladder or a rickety chair, no doubt. Take a slip on the way up with this thing and something's gonna give.

Hang the bag so the label or target is at a good level for both head and body shots.

Another Option:
Freestanding Punching Pillar

Freestanding "bags" sit on the floor and have heavy foundations to keep you from sending them through the wall. It eliminates the need to hang something and perhaps is a better option for those who rent apartments or who have limited space. They have a different sway action than a bag — moving more at the top than the bottom — thus affecting the timing of your punches.

Both will do the job — provide a good punching surface for your drills — however, I prefer the hanging bag because I can get in closer (no foundation or base in the way). I also like the feel of my punches on it and the sway seems to be a better fit for my routine.

More pillar negatory: they're more expensive than bags. I keep knocking them off their adjustment and finally, they just don't carry the right aura (what sounds better to you: Working the pillar or working the bag?).

Preparation for the Heavy Bag: Wraps

You'll wreck your hands without wraps and bag gloves. There are a zillion small bones, easily bruised or broken, in your hands and wrists that must be properly protected and supported. What's boxing without good hands?

Start the wrap with three or four turns on the wrist. I like these to be fairly snug. Next, wrap around the knuckles. Wrap with fingers spread in order to prevent squeezing when you make a fist. Make four or five not-too-snug turns here. Come back down to the thumb and make a snug wrap around it. Then take the wrap up and around the opposite side of the hand and begin making

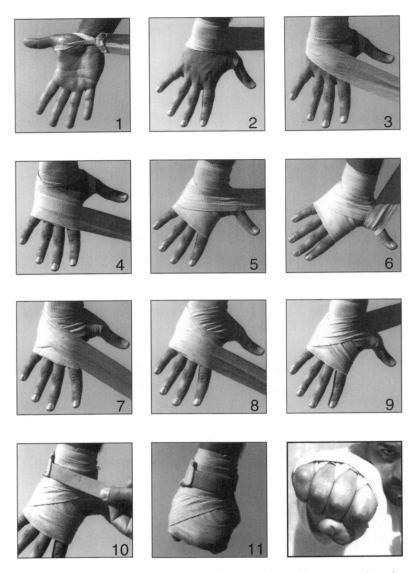

Basic wrap: Hook thumb, wrap wrist, wrap knuckles, wrap thumb, cross wrap, wrap knuckles again and tie off at wrist. Wraps protect the hands and help provide a snug glove fit.

In the last photo, Alan shows a style that includes a wrap between each finger. These wraps are made between steps 6 and 7.

an X over the hand with several not-too-snugs. As you reach the end of your wrap, bring the remainder around the wrist and tie it off. I use the models with Velcro ties, which are the easiest and most convenient.

Another method includes wrapping between each finger after securing the thumb and before you make the X. Wrap between each finger and around the base of the thumb, then come around from the other side and cross it with several wraps until you have just enough left to secure at the wrist as before. Again, make sure you wrap with your fingers spread.

I've used both wraps and prefer the finger wrapping style because it provides a more snug support.

Don't make the wraps so tight that they crimp your hand. It'll hurt like the devil when you start hitting the bag.

Putting on the Gloves

Dig your hands deep into the gloves to secure a good fit. With the wraps, your gloves should feel snug and comfortable on your hands. If your gloves have Velcro straps, you can tie off without help. You're ready to throw your first punch!

Hitting the Bag

There is some technique involved in striking the bag. Make sure you always hit the bag flush with the front of your fist. Hitting the bag with the top of your fist (it happens) causes a real owie. Hit the bag in the middle of its

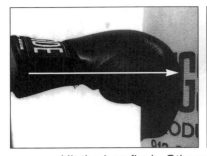

Hit the bag flush. Otherwise you'll gain a sprain.

Work with the movement of the bag. When it swings side-to-side use the hook.

When it swings straight (below) use straight punches.

Meet the bag ...   ... with the punch.

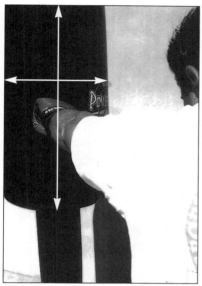

Hit the bag or pillar dead-on as it moves toward you.

horizontal axis in order to prevent it from spinning. Hit the bag as it returns to the bottom of its arc. If you hit it when it's moving away you will cause the swing to accelerate and/or you may miss entirely and hyper-extend your arm (and that hurts).

Use straight punches as the bag swings toward you and hooks if the bag moves side-to-side. Short, snappy punches applied at the right moments during the arc of the swing will keep the movement of the bag manageable.

If you punch as the bag moves away from you, you'll either miss and throw yourself off balance or cause the bag to accelerate out of control.

Determining punching distance.

Jabs First

What else? First of all, determine your punching distance to the bag. Extend your left arm so that your glove mashes into the bag when it's motionless and settle into a boxer's stance. There you go.

Snap off a jab or two at a head-high target in the middle of the bag. Your punches should crack solidly as they land and make the bag swing slightly and directly away from you without spinning.

If it's spinning you're off target. If the bag is really swinging you're pushing your punches. Remember, your jab should SNAP! -- accelerate, WHAP!, recover. You almost pull the punch. There is no follow through (as in, say, a golf swing). The sound and feel of the punch on the bag will tell you if you're hitting properly. It's a sweet feel -- like a ball on a bat. WHAP! WHAP! WHAP!

At first, practice your jabs from a solid stance to groove your form. Throughout the punch you should be balanced and in control.

Try double and triple jabs, bringing your glove all the way back to guard after each punch. Feel that deltoid burn. Work on quickness and accuracy with and without power. Keep your right arm in tight and twist your hips a bit with the punching action to deliver stiffer jabs.

Jabbing with Footwork and Rhythm

After you've jabbed from a static position for a while, try incorporating movement. Step into your jab going forward and side-to-side. Shoot the jab as the left foot lands. In between punches and steps, try your boogie-woogie rhythm. Get into it. Try to blend the punches with the steps with the rhythm with the action of the bag. Find the beat in the drill.

Stepping in with the jab. Step and punch are simultaneous. The step adds power as does a twist of the hips upon delivery.

Straight Right

Strike the bag head high using the technique described previously. Punch straight from the chin off a pivoting right foot -- swinging hips and back into the effort. Like the jab (and all punches!) think: accelerate, WHOMP! and recover. The WHOMP! indicates the deep sound of the harder blow -- your right should really rock the bag. Remember to pull the punch upon impact in order to get that SNAP! thing going and to prevent the bag from swaying wildly after each right hand delivery.

Left Hook

You need to get in close to practice the hook. It's easier to hit the bag with the palm turned in. With your weight transferring from left to right, remember to crush the peanuts with a pivoting left foot as you swing hook, torso and hips -- as a single unit -- in a powerful horizontal movement. Accelerate, SNAP! and recover to the balanced boxer's stance. You'll be booming the bag as you did with the right when you're throwing the hook correctly.

To practice left hooks to the body lower yourself by flexing your knees.

Remember not to wind up with the left hook. It's a compact punch thrown within the body frame powered by a twisting torso.

Uppercuts

Get in close to land either left or right uppercuts. Dip the shoulder and drive these punches from the hip -- again without winding up.

Straight Right

Left Uppercut

Left Hook

Multi-jabs

Remember to fully recover after each blow. Try to keep power consistent from the first to the last jab in each combination.

One-Two

Don't let up or cheat on the jab just to unload on a booming right hand. Keep the jab snappy. Make sure you recover the jab fully before you throw the right.

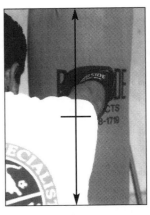

One-Two-Three

Align your right shoulder to the horizontal center of the bag before you begin in order to properly attack the bag from both sides.

Since the hook requires a shorter punching distance than the jab and the right, you'll need to compromise your boxing distance somewhat. Step in with the jab, land a shorter right, come off the weight transfer with a snappy left and step back out again. Don't forget to throw a strong jab because you're anticipating the power punches that follow. Work especially on the transition from right to left. And try not to get too frustrated by your sloppy left hook. Remember to bring your hands back to your chin after every punch. Beware of the droopy right hand. Got all that?

Right-Left, Left-Right

Get up close and align your right shoulder to the center of the bag. Your right will be a little stubby in order to

One-Two-Three

accommodate the left hook. This combination is all about working off the natural weight transfer inherent in each punch. The right flows into your left which flows into your right, etc. Think pivoting feet, crushed peanuts and short, compact punches. Start with the right at times and sometimes with the left hook.

Keep the punches coming in a steady, even beat throughout each combination -- BOOM! BOOM! BOOM! Don't develop hiccups in your delivery -- BOOM, boom ... BOOM!

Moving with the Bag
Move in, out and around the bag as you work your stuff. Use the steps and the rhythm. Learn how to move as you deliver solid blows. Keep your steps short, your stance balanced and your rhythm fluid.

The Hardest Thing
Stepping up and back with your combinations is the hardest doggone thing. However, in a bout it's vitally important to know how to fight on the move since most of the time you are continually in motion. Basically the move involves stepping with the hand that throws -- right foot with right hand and left foot with left hand. It's a simple concept but difficult to coordinate. Practice by shuffling up and back executing a loose one-two combination to get a feel for the foot-to-hand feeling. Use half steps. Going back is harder than moving forward.

Refine your punching technique as you develop coordination. The heavy bag can be utilized up to a point. You can practice this drill moving into the bag but not away from it.

Moving with the bag.

Basic Defense & Counters

Boxing is 50% offense and 50% defense. That's not so easy to see when you're pounding the heavy bag all by yourself and checking out your oh-so-pretty punching technique in the mirror.

What You Already Know
The boxer's stance provides a great deal of protection unto itself: chin is tucked, hands are held high to protect the head, arms are arranged to protect the lower torso, feet are well apart and knees are flexed to provide a balanced and easily mobile athletic posture. Add footwork and head movement and not only can you survive an opponent's initial attack, but you'll be a hard target to hit.

Basic stuff yet easily forgotten. How many boxers have suffered from ignoring the fundamentals: leaving a chin exposed ... dropping the hands late in a bout ... standing stock still in an opponent's striking zone ... getting caught off balance ... or simply losing eye contact? Like they say, *keep the chin down and the guard up,* and you'll prevent disaster a large percentage of the time.

However, boxing like a dancing turtle will not help you score or even survive for very long against a capable opponent.

 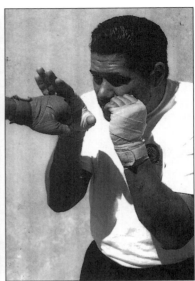

Jab Catching

As a left jab arrives, place your right glove in front of your face with chin down. Pivot your right foot, brace the right leg and catch the jab in your glove. Make sure your chin is down so your glove bounces off your forehead and not your nose. Catch jabs as aggressively as your opponent throws them. Recover immediately.

Parries

It's not a good idea to catch a straight right. Power punches are best parried with a small slap of the left glove where the momentum can carry your opponent off balance and expose him to a counterpunch.

Parrying Body Shots

Punches to the body can be parried by sweeping an arm and deflecting the punch outside, while pivoting and sliding in the opposite direction of the punch.

Parry a straight right to the head with a tap of the left hand. The parry deflects the punch. It doesn't stop it.

Parry a right to the body with an outside sweep of the left arm.

Alison blocks a right hook to the head with a slight flex of the knees which brings up her guard.

Note the eye contact. Never take your eyes off your opponent.

Duck with a flex at the knees. Keep your head up and your guard in place.

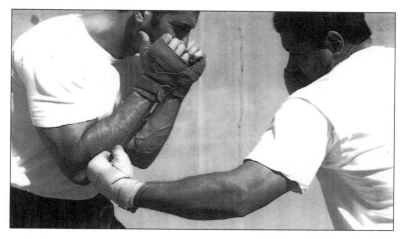

Blocks

As a punch arrives, simply flex the knees and lower yourself so that hands automatically are raised to better protect the head. At the same time elbows and arms drop to better protect the lower body. This is not a full-on duck but a somewhat slight flexing of knees. Immediately recover to the boxer's stance.

Ducks

Ducks are executed by flexing at the knees and coming up in the opposite direction of any punch in a **V** movement (this should put you in position to counter into your opponent's exposed area). Don't bend at the hips and lose eye contact with your opponent. Keep your hands up throughout the maneuver. Recover immediately.

Slips

Small, sideways movements of the head that dodge the bullet are called slips. It takes a keen eye to spot the incoming missile and a talented set of neck muscles to maneuver the head out of the way. A master of the slip was an early Mike Tyson.

A good way to practice slips is by dodging the weighted end of a swinging rope, preferably in front of a mirror. With the knot or weight hung at eye level, give it a push so that it swings to and fro at your head. Practice dodging the rope using smallish, efficient "slips" of the head. Slips are neck and head propelled. They aren't ducks or shoulder dips.

Get good at this. It's one of the best ways to deal with incoming punches since the defensive intent is to avoid the attack all together (versus a block or a catch that absorbs). The action is also relatively slight and less drastic than a duck, which of course, takes more energy and moves you out of your stance.

Inside slip   Guard position   Outside slip

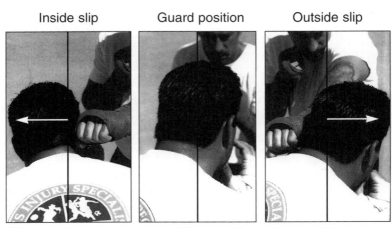

Slips are slight movements of the head to avoid straight punches.

Counterpunching

Immediately after a block, slip or duck, fire your punch into your opponent's exposed area. The following pages show examples of some basic counters to the jab, straight right and left hook.

Reaction Punching

Definitely blurs the line between offense and defense. This is a faster, more advanced type of counterpunching based on reacting to your opponent's punch and throwing into the exposed target that his punch creates. It takes courage and finely tuned reflexes to throw into a punch. You can't flinch and pull your punches during a counterattack. As with all your punches you gotta see 'em through. Even if they don't land clean, chances are you'll at least disrupt the attack.

Range & Refuge

Know your opponent's boxing distance. If you're outside his striking zone, you can't get hit.

Another safe place to be is inside your opponent's chest, believe it or not. How can he hit you? It's a great place to duck a straight right, and even too close for him to land a hook. But don't shell up in there. Keep your eyes on your opponent and recover immediately.

Offense as Defense

If you lay back, your opponent will build confidence in his punches and gain the initiative. You gotta throw to keep him honest and to create confidence in your own punches.

Counters to the jab

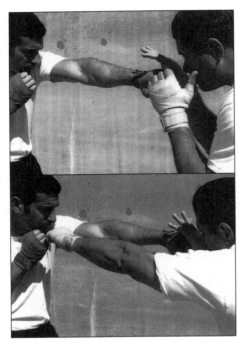

Alan catches Lance's jab ...

... and counters with his own jab.

Catching the jab and reacting with a straight right over the top. A right counter will easily overcome the jab.

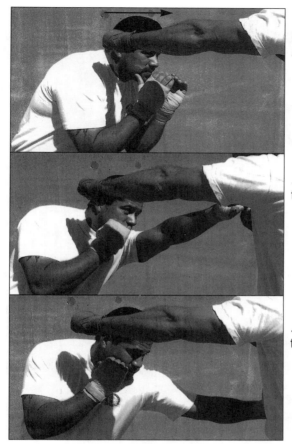

Slipping inside, Alan can counter ...

... with a left jab to the head ...

... or a left hook to the body.

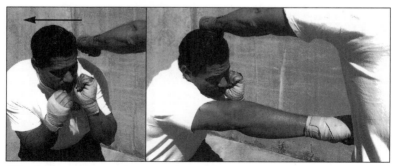

Slipping outside and countering with a straight right.

Counters to the <u>straight right</u>

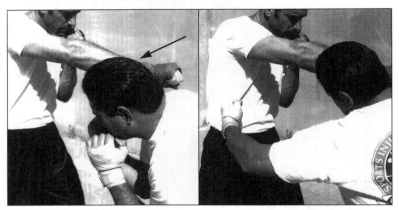

Alan slips outside and counters with a left hook to the body.

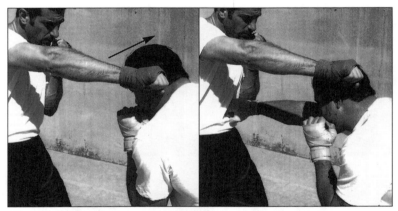

Slipping inside and countering with a right to the body.

Parring and countering with a jab over the top.

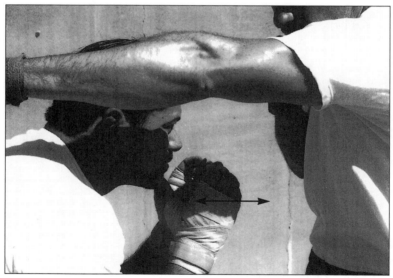

Inside the striking zone. Alan is too close for Lance to effectively land an attack.

Counters to the <u>left hook</u>

Alan blocks the hook and with the same hand reacts with a straight right to the exposed target.

Ducking outside and countering with a right to the body.

Blocking and rolling with Lance's left and coming back with his own left hook.

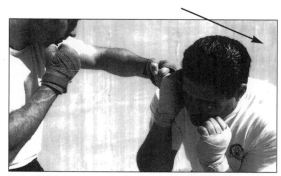

Some Major Defensive Points:

Keep your **eyes on your opponent.**

Keep your **guard up.**

Keep your **chin down.**

Keep moving when you're in the strike zone.

Don't lunge your punches.

After every action **recover immediately** to guard.

Don't lean back to avoid punches.

Give as much as you take.

Don't get mad -- step back, settle down, get smart.

Don't be predictable -- **mix up your fight plan.**

Shadowboxing: Now Include Defense

Include the defensive with the offensive in your shadowboxing routine. Practice your blocks, slips and ducks with your various punches and punch combinations.

Defense and offense are hardly separate and distinct actions in a bout. One blends into the other or should. Each punch comes from and returns to a defensive posture. Each defensive maneuver can lead to an attack. It's a swirling, flowing thing and it takes training to react properly and quickly at the right time.

Chapter Eight:

Punch Mitts: Working
Offense with Defense

Hitting Something with a Brain

Punch mitts are pads that strap on the hands. Your training coach or partner wears them as targets for your punches and can be used to simulate return fire. It's a step up from bag work since your target is capable of thinking, moving and reacting to your actions. And unlike your bag, your target talks (and grunts) back. Since the targets are small, punch mitt drills also develop accuracy.

All the stuff you work into the heavy bag can be brought to your punch mitt drills. Punches and combinations can be practiced standing still as well as moving up and back with rhythm (as you would during actual sparring). Also, punch mitts can be gently thrown to simulate incoming punches and combinations in order to work on your defensive game. Practice blocks, parries, slips, ducks, counterpunches and reaction punches.

As you can see the punch mitts allow you to work on offense and defense during the same drill or set of drills. For example, throw a jab at one hand and a right at the other, duck a left hook and come back with another right. It takes some coordination between the puncher and the catcher, but it's possible to simulate specific offensive and defensive encounters very much like the real thing. The advantage, of course, is that nobody is really taking any shots outside of a low flying punch mitt (which shouldn't be thrown with much intent in the first place). And, of course, you gotta remember to throw at your partner's mitts and not his face.

Punch mitts or focus pads provide a bridge between training alone on the heavy bag and sparring.

Counterclockwise from the top, Teri delivers a 1-2-3 combination.

The mitts are more than punch pads. They can be used to simulate offensive action such as this left to the body.

After the successful block, Katrina counters with a right hook.

All the counters demonstrated earlier can be drilled with the mitts.

In this sequence Alison is drilling her skills as a range fighter – stepping in with the jab, then stepping back out of range.

Ducking down and up in a **V** in the direction of the punch. The dotted line indicates her final destination.

Working her slips.
Note the eye contact.

Successful slips
entail just the
slightest movement
of the head.

Semi-Sparring

A tick below full-on sparring has your coach or partner wearing a punch mitt on his right hand and a sparring glove on his left. You must wear headgear and a mouthpiece. If you're working on defending attacks to the body, strap on your groin protector, too. Your partner will throw jabs or hooks, which you must defend against with blocks, slips and ducks. You will try to score with jabs and rights on his punch mitt.

I know this sounds grossly unfair (and it pretty much is) but again the idea here is to work on things. Your partner is throwing at 3/4 speed with zero intent. You are working on your complete game — footwork, defense and offense. The idea is to avoid punches and at the same time to set up your own attacks. For example, as you block or slip a punch, think in terms of coming off that block or slip with a counter. Remember boxing is a constant flow between offensive and defensive action and this drill makes you very, very aware of that. The action doesn't stop after one terrific punch or slip. It keeps roaring along and you gotta keep up.

Getting Hit

Although these drills are most definitely intended to be light offensive/defensive exercises, you're gonna get hit. If your training takes you in this direction, this is when you'll experience your first tap. It should be a light tap as the intent here is to learn, but a light tap to one man is a wrecking ball to another. And in the heat of the action (and it can get hot) things happen. That's why you should train with an accredited coach. You are a beginner and need to know that your partner is not gonna go out of control. You also need a partner who can control you.

Now, about taking your first punch. Everyone has a tolerance level, and you'll know right away where yours is. It's not a guessing game. Some folks are OK with it and some aren't. Personally, I think the light stuff mentioned here is no worse than falling down while skiing, snowboarding

Getting nailed is a shock and maddening at first. However, it is something you can learn to deal with. Just make sure you're using the proper gear!

or in-line skating. I've hurt myself doing these things and dealt with it. Of course, boxing is boxing and there's a steady stream of punishment involved at the competitive level, but that's something else entirely and I'm not going there.

To be specific, the worst I received during the semi-sparring is a sore nose (not busted), a bruised rib and a slight headache. The rib was a drag because it hurt for a week and made it difficult to lie down. Compared to the punishment I've endured with snowboarding and roller hockey, however, this ain't no big thing.

Flinching

Flinching is a very natural reaction when you see the missiles approach but a poor habit to acquire in boxing. Work on keeping your eyes open and on your opponent no matter what.

And flinching is more than winking eyelids. It's also pulling punches before they reach a target when you see one coming. It's better to finish the punch since it may still land or at least disrupt the incoming missile.

Happy Feet

Happy feet are common in sparring. It's especially common to bounce backward and around and around. It's wise to block the back foot during punch mitt drills to clip the tendency.

Hey, Relax

Boxing is about relaxation and explosive action. Boxers must learn to relax between punches in order to conserve energy. Nothing takes it out of you like unrelieved, tense muscles over the course of a round.

Chapter Nine:

Boxer's Workout

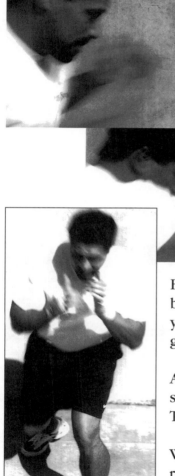

Shadowbox to smooth out form and develop technique.

Forty to 60 minutes of the boxer's workout will cleanse your psyche and lay you out. It's good medicine. The best.

Arrive in sneakers, athletic socks, shorts or sweats and T-shirt.

Wrap your hands. You don't really need to right away, but it sets a routine and establishes in your mind that you are, after all, a boxer.

Shadowboxing

Run through your shadowboxing routine. Include stance, footwork and rhythm, punches, combinations and defensive maneuvers. This is a warm up and a chance to examine form.

While looking at yourself in the mirror, start each drill slowly and gradually build speed:

Stepping in four directions

Long and short rhythm

Jabs

Straight right and left hooks

Uppercuts

One-two combinations

One-two-three combinations

Jabs with stepping

Rights and hooks with blocks, slips and ducks

Rights and hooks stepping up and back

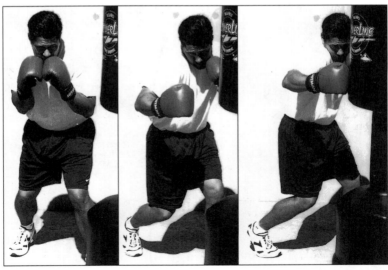

Work the bag as if it's a real opponent. Pretend you're defending against and countering a variety of attacks.

Heavy Bag

With one minute rests in between, go three minute rounds each of:
Jabs
One-twos
One-two-threes
Right-lefts, Left-rights
Free form outside fighting (moving in, out and around)
Free form inside fighting (staying inside, lots of side-to-side motion)

Skipping Rope

Skipping rope is great exercise by itself. It's fun, aerobic and builds coordination:
100 skips with both feet
Alternating with two feet, right foot and left foot:
10 reps of each, then 9, 8, 7, 6, 5, 4, 3, 2, 1
Try running in place and skipping
Try combining running with a side to side swinging
Try backwards skipping
Try double jumps

Terri alternates feet, runs in place and skips with both feet. Skipping rope is great exercise and a terrific coordination drill.

Sparring is great fun.
Putting all that training into real action is exciting stuff.

Chapter Ten:

Sparring

Hard and Fast

The bag doesn't punch back. Focus mitts go pitty-pat. A sparring partner is required for you to learn true action/reaction. Your boxing education at this stage comes hard and fast. Make sure you're ready for it and that you do it right.

Geared Up: Make sure you always wear proper head gear, mouthpiece, training gloves and groin protection when you spar.

Coach

The wild-ass nature of combat requires supervision. Somebody needs to control the efforts of you and your partner and it should be your coach. Or spar with your coach. Find a good one and listen to him. Your coach is your boxing education.

Safety First

Spar with protective gear. Spar with proper supervision. Spar with intent to learn.

Initial Training

Sparring is intense. It's an adrenaline-drenched, crashing, almost dream-like experience. Hey, it's combat. Just you and the other guy looking for a shot. Maybe you think some, but for the most part it's action, reaction.

Concentrate on eye contact at all times.

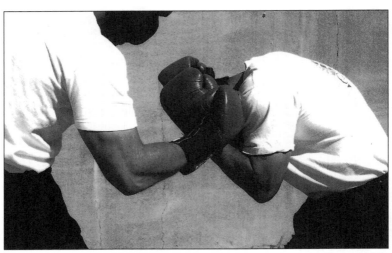

Shelling up is a very sane response to an attack and will probably be one of the first things you'll do out there. However, it's wiser to keep your eyes on your attacker and develop a more sophisticated defense.

Pawing is a common beginner's error that leaves half the head exposed. Never paw or reach. Learn to throw crisp punches that snap back to guard.

Your performance is a direct product of your training. It's not enough to know what to do in your head. You gotta know in your hands and legs. Hence the need for a long, sustained training period before your first bout.

Go Easy
It's wise to adopt an easy-does-it approach to sparring. Learning how to hit and take hits in live action takes some getting used to. Just swinging away without purpose is no good. It won't be boxing, it won't be safe and it won't be much fun. There's simply no point to it.

Plans
Your initial sparring should be highly controlled learning sessions. You're working stuff out, not trying to beat somebody up. Go into these practice bouts with simple game plans. Work on specific things. Perhaps during one round you'd like to sharpen your jab and use alotta slips. During another round try a lead right and certain counterpunches. Pick one or two offensive things and one or two defensive things. Keep it manageable in your mind. Otherwise it'll become a brawl. Why all the training if you're just gonna throw it all away in a free-for-all? You want to build yourself into something.

Flow
Sparring is an opportunity to try out those things you've been applying to the bag and punching mitts. Of course, the other guy won't be standing still because he'll have his own game plan. All those skills that looked so pretty in practice won't come off exactly as planned. Maybe they won't come off at all. You and your sparring partner will create your own little world of boxing in three-minute, action-packed chunks of time. Go with the flow.

Squaring off to your opponent provides him with a much larger target and eliminates your balance and mobility. Note that Alan is literally back on his heels.

Under the same attack, Alan maintains his boxer's stance and is able to slip inside Lance's right hand without loss of balance, mobility or initiative. In fact, he's in perfect position to counter with his right.

Composure

It takes time to get used to getting hit. At first you may get mad and want revenge at any cost but that's not the point. Better to figure out why you got hit (there's always a reason) and improve upon the weakness in your defense. Your anger will impede your growth as a boxer. Composure is absolutely crucial at all times and key to success. Even more so when your nose throbs and your pride is pounded.

Review

Watching videos of your performances will enhance your education immeasurably. Seeing is believing. See how your guard drops. See how awful your footwork is. See how slow your reactions are. When you're mixing it up it's hard to tell what's going on. You can get the wrong idea. But the clips will tell you true. Review your bouts and your learning will sprout wheels.

The upper jab is a nifty trick. It starts with a dropped left that invites an attack. As the opponent steps in, flex your knees and swing up and underneath his punch. It can be a big surprise.

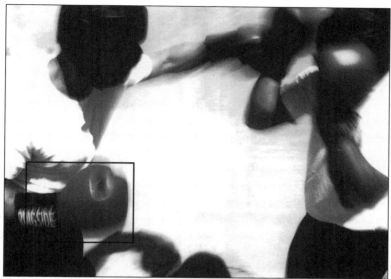

The first thing that goes in the heat of battle is your guard. Above, Lance's right hand has fallen to his waist leaving him wide open for Alan's left. It takes alotta training to keep the hands up at all times. In the photo below, note that Alan's right hand is glued to his cheek as he delivers his jab. He's fully protected from a counter and at the same time ready to throw with it.

Inside fighting requires swift and sure head movement and a mastery of counterpunching in order to penetrate and deliver an effective attack. Alan steps in, ducks a right and counters with a left uppercut as he blocks and rolls off a left hook.

Outside or range fighting makes use of distance in order to deliver quick offensive forays. It takes timing and speedy footwork to get in and out effectively.

Start-Up Sparring: Common Problems:

Squaring off to an opponent (planting your feet directly in front of an opponent so that you face him with your chest). Never compromise your basic defensive posture.

Signaling intentions with shoulders, head or flying elbow before your punch is thrown. Deliver your punches crisply and cleanly. Straight punches fire directly from chin to target.

Predictability with movements or offensive and defensive style. A boxer must mix up his approach so that his opponent won't see patterns.

Reaching and pawing. These are largely useless actions that will expose you to dangerous counters.

Hesitation. Finish your punches. They may land or disrupt the counter. Half a punch is worthless.

Flinching. Learn to keep your eyes on your opponent – even under fire!

Fatigue. It takes time and training to build stamina.

Slow and sloppy technique. It also takes time and training to groove your offensive and defensive actions.

Nervous prancing and bouncing. Happy feet happen naturally and must be curbed to conserve energy.

Inability to relax between actions. The intensity of sparring makes it hard to relax out there, but relax you must, in order to conserve energy and to execute technique properly.

Anger. Has no place in sparring.

Charging. Usually the result of frustration. With an experienced opponent you'll be cut down in no time.

Chapter Eleven:

History

Love & Hate in America, Amateurs vs. Pros & the Champs

Ancient Stuff

Art from ancient Egypt and Crete shows athletic looking fellows throwing what appear to be punches at each other. The Greeks refined the pursuit and included boxing in their Olympic Games. Art on vases and sculpture as well as extensive tournament records reveal a highly sophisticated sport that included great champions and epic fights, organized and refereed matches, hand wraps (maybe even gloves) and perhaps the beginning of modern punching technique.

Rome took up the sport with a nasty twist. The hand wraps were studded to inflict immediate and lethal harm. One clean punch and it was over. Boxing in Rome was a gladiator event pursued by slaves for the blood lust of those in the stadium seats. Needless to say, these events didn't encourage technique, refinement or sportsmanship. What little science gained was lost. And like a lot of things that first appeared in ancient Greece and Rome, boxing disappeared for a very, very long time.

From Swords to Knuckles

The sport finally reappeared in England in the early 1700s. Curiously, boxing was cultivated in the fencing establishments which were very big then (all gentlemen learned how to fence). Boxing was considered the "gentle" art of self defense (fists being gentler than steel) and often taught by the same master. The influence of fencing can be seen particularly in the early boxing stance which included a straight back and a wide, sideways stance with one arm leading.

Boxing was a bare knuckle affair at this time and remained so for almost another 200 years. The sport became popular across the board and drew large crowds who loved to gamble and watch the bloodletting. In the beginning it was all so brutally simple. Rich patrons (eventually, even royalty) backed likely candidates and pitted them against each other wherever they could do so legally.

From Gouging to Gloves

Rules were spare. At first there really weren't any. Guys just faced each other and slugged, kicked, bit and gouged away until only one was left standing. Technique wasn't much either. Except for a notable exception or two, boxers squared off and bashed away.

In 1741, things got a bit more polished with a set of rules created by Jack Broughton after he killed an opponent in the ring. Rounds were created based on knockdowns — once a man went down he had 30 seconds to get back up. Once he did, another round began. Since there were no time limits, fights sometimes lasted hours. You couldn't hit a man if he was down or wrestle below the waist. Broughton is also credited with developing basic boxing skills including blocking and retreating.

Almost 100 years later another boxing death led to a safer set of rules. In 1838 the Pugilists' Protective Association of London created the London Prize Ring Rules which were revised in 1853 and again in 1866.

In the 1850s the concept of weight classes was born. Until then it was usually just the two biggest brawlers in town (although it should be noted that talented smaller fellows sometimes rocked the giants). At first the divisions were simply lightweight, middleweight and heavyweight. By 1910 there were nine divisions. Today there are seventeen classes in professional boxing and twelve recognized by United States Amateur Boxing, Inc. (USA Boxing, Inc.).

In 1866 the Marquess of Queensbury created the rules that revolutionized boxing. The Queensbury Rules:
1) Included a ban on wrestling.
2) Indicated that rounds should last three minutes with a one-minute break in between.
3) Stated that gloves must be worn.
4) Stipulated that fights should last no more than 20 rounds.
5) Later included a scoring system based on each fighter's performance.

America's Love/Hate Relationship with Boxing
America imported the sport through barnstorming English boxers, Irish immigrants and perhaps through the sons of rich American southerners who had gone to England for their education. It's thought that perhaps the latter introduced their slaves to boxing. At any rate, by the mid-1800s boxing was off and running in the United States. By the turn of the century America owned it for good.

As in England, the excitement of fistfighting (and the gambling that seemed to be such an integral part of it) proved to be very popular with everyone except those of a puritanical bent. To this day the tug of war between the allure and revulsion of two men hitting each other has molded the history of boxing -- particularly prize fighting or professional boxing. Issues of legality, morality and race have defined, influenced and plagued the sport every step of the way.

White Hat, Black Hat: Amateur vs. Professional

In 1880 the Amateur Boxing Association (ABA) was established in England. This was the forerunner of numerous organizations that organize and promote amateur boxing and boxing competition for all age groups. The United States Amateur Boxing, Inc. (USA Boxing -- formerly known as the United States Amateur Boxing Federation) -- has governed men's (and now women's) amateur boxing in the United States since 1888.

It should be strongly noted at this point that the paths of professional and amateur boxing took different directions, and today stand in sharp contrast with each other. Although the professional ranks are, by and large, replenished from amateurs, the boxing that they each represent is altogether different.

The intent of amateur boxing is to showcase boxing skills. Scoring is based on all punches that land cleanly. The force of those blows or their effect doesn't count (haymakers score the same as jabs). Bouts are short and carefully supervised. Boxers wear protective headgear (since 1948) as well as specially designed gloves. Safety is a major concern.

The professionals showcase boxing and slugging. Although a skillful fighter is appreciated, throughout time fans have always wanted to see fierce, unfettered combat -- knockdowns and knockouts are the ultimate goals. Boxers don't wear headgear and their gloves are lighter and more lethal than those of the amateurs. Safety is certainly less of a concern.

And then there's the money, the gambling, the criminals, the corrupt politicians and the fighters on the take. Prizefighting has always been strongly influenced if not controlled by darker forces and oddly enough (this is the 21st century, isn't it?) it doesn't look like that'll ever change. Some have suggested that the corruption is actually an integral part of boxing's appeal -- like it adds drama and color or some such thing. The theory makes a little sense. Gangsters have influenced mainstream fashion, language and entertainment since day one. Rubbing shoulders with the bad boys is sorta cool. Sometimes. I guess.

On the other hand, amateur boxing is highly organized with a strong tradition of sportsmanship (we are talking *Olympic* style boxing here) with no monetary gain. Overshadowed by prizefighting, the public is hardly aware of its existence outside of the Olympic Games every four years (where so many of the celebrated first shone --- Ali, Foreman, Frazier, Patterson, Leonard, Holyfield ...). But it's there, all right. And there are all kinds of great things about it: upright organizations and contests, certified coaching, outstanding athletic achievements and people having fun.

Champs
Whether or not something can be or should be done with the pros is outside the scope of this book.

However, for better or worse the pros have always held the limelight and the heavyweight champion, in particular, has held a mighty position in our culture for more than 100 years. After all, when they say "Champ" they ain't talking about the world's greatest hitter, passer or hoopsman -- the Champ is the Heavyweight Champion of the World.

Briefly, some very notable World Heavyweight Champions:

The modern era of boxing was ushered in with the legendary **John L. Sullivan.** He was the first boxing hero in the United States and the first World Champion in 1882. He fought the last bare-knuckle championship and the first one with gloves. He was the guy who said, "I can lick any son of a bitch in the house!" and usually did. He was a genuine public hero and almost by himself launched boxing into the new century.

In 1892, **Gentleman Jim Corbett** beat John L. with footwork and strategy. Although he was never forgiven for whipping an icon, his boxing style was the start of something new.

Bob Fitzsimmons was born in England, raised in New Zealand and started his fighting career in Australia. He won world middleweight, light-heavyweight and heavyweight titles with a fighting weight of less than 160 pounds. In 1899 he lost his heavyweight title to James Jeffries who outweighed him by nearly 60 pounds (by the 11th round Fitzsimmons had broken both hands on the large man's skull and fell defenseless).

Fitz's classic quote before that fight: "The bigger they are, the harder they fall."

In 1908 **Jack Johnson** became heavyweight champion and one of the great ones to boot. But he was black, brash and slept with a white woman. Back then this was like a visitation from the Anti-Christ. It laid open America's ugly, seething struggle with race, and combined with the anti-boxing elements at work, knocked the sport full on its backside. Because of the swirling mess associated with this guy, black fighters (especially heavyweights) were ignored and denied meaningful opportunity for years. This is where all that Great White Hope business originated.

Then there was **Jack Dempsey.** All the pieces of his saga fell together perfectly to create one of the greatest legends in sports history. The right tale (from rags to riches — an American story of success), the right face (rugged, handsome, mean), the right promoter (Tex Rickard, mastermind of the first million-dollar gate), the right race (white), the right decade (the roaring '20s) and the right fighter (a killer with bombs in both hands). After the First World War, America was ready to close in on itself and have some fun. And Jack Dempsey, along with Babe Ruth and Red Grange, gave it to 'em, baby.

Gene Tunney beat Dempsey twice in two titanic bouts. He did it with his head, skill and training. He was a boxer's boxer, a gentleman and another rags to riches fighter who fathered a United States Senator after he hung up his gloves.

Joe Lewis is considered one of the greats of all time and during his tenure was probably the most celebrated black man on earth. He was carefully groomed for his role because the idea of a black champion was still very tricky. Unlike Jack Johnson, Lewis remained quiet, polite and avoided white women. His bout with the German Max Schmedding in 1938 was epic beyond anything Hollywood could ever dream up. He demolished Hitler's chosen champion in one round with an adoring America glued to the radio. Lewis dominated boxing from 1937 to 1949 (including four years in the Army) and defended his title more than any other heavyweight in history.

Lewis's famous warning to a backpeddling opponent: "You can run but you can't hide."

Rocky Marciano won every one of his 49 professional bouts. No other heavyweight champion has retired undefeated. He reigned supreme from 1952 through 1956 and owned a knockout percentage of .877! The real Rocky is on everyone's list of all-time greats.

Muhammad Ali was the definition of power, grace and speed. He was also intelligent, courageous and fantastically entertaining. He won the heavyweight crown three times and fought in some of the most celebrated fights ever. He was highly controversial, yet became one of the most popular men on earth. He was first crowned in 1964, lost it in 1967 because he refused to join the Army over religious convictions, won it again in 1974 (against a humorless George Foreman), lost it in 1978 to Leon Spinks but won it back shortly thereafter. It can be said that Ali was boxing from 1964 to 1979.

Ali's all-time line: "Float like a butterfly, sting like a bee."

In 1986 a brute of a fighter burst on the scene and literally ransacked the heavyweight division. At 20, **Mike Tyson** became the youngest heavyweight champion in history and for a while it looked like the title would be his forever. But the wheel fell off the wagon in 1990 when Buster Douglas knocked him out in a stunning upset. Tyson's been more or less shooting himself in the foot ever since.

In 1987 **George Foreman**, former world heavyweight champ (1973-74), came out of retirement to earn money for his family and his church. Big and slow, he was given little chance to succeed and was something of a joke for three years, although he crushed all his opponents up to and including Gerry Cooney in 1990. He lost his world championship bid to Evander Holyfield in 1991 but finally won it all in 1995 against WBA / IBF title holder Michael Moorer.

The unlikely comeback effort of the 40-something slugger was inspirational. Big George's quick wit, wide grin and warm sense of humor captured the hearts of people everywhere — even among those who normally found boxing repugnant. The new George (the youthful Foreman was actually rather sullen) gave boxing its biggest boost since the heyday of Muhammad Ali.

Evander Holyfield overcame the odds and a host of problems including a bum heart to become a worthy and respected champion. He has defeated all challengers (most notably Iron Mike Tyson — twice) and is considered the undisputed champ as this book goes to print.

Becoming a Boxer

My boxing education has been sixty lessons and about ten sparring bouts over a span of eight months, as well as many, many hours of homework on my own.

The following journal covers a good deal of what actually went on. I didn't include every entry because it would be too long and tedious. What I have here is probably too much but there you go. It's authentic anyway. That's for sure.

I had a great coach; that's why I got this far with this project. I trained and trained before I threw and ate my first hard punch. I learned how to punch, block, slip, duck and counter. I learned how to move my head and feet in ways they've never been moved before. I jumped rope with two feet, one foot (then the other), side-to-side and running in place. I whaled away on a heavy bag in my back yard until my dogs howled and the sweat jumped off my body. I got mad every now and then and learned how to let it go. I took a shot or two and discovered it wasn't that bad. I could take it. I learned that the fear of combat could be molded into excitement and sometimes exhilaration. You can really ride it somewhere.

I wish I'd learned how to box when I was a kid. It does something for you. It gives you a physical self-confidence. You gain a robust presence. Something like a spring in your step but a little more substantial than that. Boxing can show you the way to fitness, fun and even courage. The last entry in the journal describes the experience of a young man in my sparring group who stood up to a bully with his boxing skills and won something for himself.

There's a lot right about boxing and hopefully I've made that point clear enough in these pages. I have a wonderful time with it, and I know I'm lucky to have hooked up with the right people. Thanks, Alan.

D.W. / 3-27-98

Chapter Twelve:

Boxer's Journal:
Author's Six-Month Journey

INTO THE MIX 7-24-97: Lesson #1

Big Al

I met Al during my fencing instruction earlier this year. He was a student as well and had the makings of a damn fine fencer until a bum knee forced him to drop out. Possessed with amazing speed and reflexes, it came as no surprise when he told me he used to box. He now coaches high-school football and teaches boxing also. The idea of taking boxing lessons was intriguing and for several weeks it simmered in my head until I finally realized that I really wanted to give it a try and that I better do this thing.

Al's about 30, big and powerful, yet trim and fit. He's been boxing since he was a little kid and used to compete on an amateur level (winning 90% of his fights) although he shows none of the wear and tear one might expect. He's clear and sharp with his instructions, speaks in a rapid staccato and obviously loves everything about his art. Throughout the hour-long lesson he embellishes instruction with snippets about famous fighters as well as his own experiences. He's a very good teacher.

This is a Gym?

I meet him at the gym he works out of in La Jolla (if gym is the word to use for a place populated with gorgeous women in tights. Spa? Health club? Carrot juice bar?). We shake hands and he takes me through the rows of glittering equipment to a glassed-in room off to the side. The smallish room has a big punching bag hanging from the ceiling and one of those smaller head-sized things you always see fighters effortlessly whaling away on in the movies when they're talking to reporters. One entire wall is mirrored so that I can witness every clumsy step of my lesson.

Man, I look fat.

> Putting on the gloves is a little thrilling. Like suiting up for battle or something.

Looking Good! (I Think)

We start with the wraps which are cloth strips that cover and protect the knuckles of the hand and thumb. Al has me hold my hands out, palms down, fingers spread as he wraps and wraps the longish cloth (like an Ace bandage) around each of my mitts. There's a special way to wrap and I'm expected to learn it right away so that I can do it myself. When he's done I make a fist and the wrap tightens around my hand. I look in the mirror and think *yeah it's happening*. There is no doubt. I'm a boxing student.

He shows me the stance, which is a little more complicated than I might have guessed. I settle into a surfer's stance with my left foot forward since I'm right-handed. At this point I'm sorta surfing in the direction of my imagined opponent. Then he has me place my right foot out a bit so that my right heel lines up with my left foot's toes. Then I pivot on both heels and swing my toes 45 degrees toward the target. Feet are well apart, about shoulder width, and my knees are flexed in order to assume an athletic posture.

Chin is tucked down so that I'm actually peering up. Arms are held close to the sides (like golf) with the forearms running straight up like two pillars protecting my ribs. Fists are about eye level on either side of my face and held in close. Looking into the mirror I think I look the part of a budding boxer and I'm feeling pretty frisky.

Arthur Murray Must Have Been a Middleweight

Then we move. Up and back, side to side. The lead foot leads and you never cross over. This is sorta like fencing. Up and back is easy, side to side is trickier, especially going frontside which feels (and looks) like lumbering. I'm told that's normal and why most fighters like to move to their backside versus their frontside. I'm doing OK with all this ... three steps up ... three steps back ... three steps backside ... three steps frontside ... then Al introduces rhythm.

Boxers never stand stock still. Even when they aren't traveling they must bob or rock from foot to foot in order to maintain a state of readiness and not to become sitting ducks (it's harder to hit a moving target). Al says you simply can't box well from a static position. You must keep a rhythm going. And it's exactly like learning a dance step, especially when you try to move between bobs (you stop bobbing when you step and immediately resume bobbing when you stop stepping).

I do all right with this, although at times, I flounder and lead with the wrong foot. For the first time I feel silly and a little clumsy. Of course the mirror is right there broadcasting all my shuffling about and I'm briefly reminded of my darkest hours at Arthur Murray's Dance Studio (I swear my wife made me go!). Al is very happy with my stumbling efforts, however, and says it's time for the gloves.

The Ritual

Up to this point I've been wearing only the wraps. Al goes over to a box full of gloves, pulls out one, opens it up and says push straight down and in. I poke my hand in and he secures the Velcro strap (I'm thinking where are the laces? The last time I wore boxing gloves I was 12 years old and I had to lace, not strap). He puts the other one on me and I'm complete. I look in the mirror and (oh my!) I look like a boxer. Putting on the gloves is a little thrilling. Like suiting up for battle or something.

Each glove weighs 12 ounces and has an interesting thumb design that pieces into the fat or hand part of the mitt. The top of the gloved thumb is attached to the rest of the glove in order to prevent the thumb from sticking out and getting broken or poking an opponent's eye.

The Jab

After the strapping-in ritual, Al shows me how to jab. Jabbing is a straight-from-the-shoulder, popping action into your opponent's face accomplished with your leading hand. Al says a good boxer must develop a good jab for a number of reasons. It's the punch you will throw the most. It's used to set up the big money punch with your other (more powerful) hand. Jabbing is an offensive action that doesn't sacrifice the defensive position (it's a punch you can throw without breaking your boxer's stance and recover from quickly). The jab is this important: Al says that his first coach tied his right

arm up for two months in order to force him to develop his jab.

He goes on to say that in a street fight, it's the only punch he'll use. Without the gloves, a jab is lethal enough to break a nose. Thus his other hand can play a defensive role only.

Al straps flat practice pads on his hands and has me jab at the target dots on each. The punch should be thrown from a relaxed state. In fact, as I'm in my boxer's stance, the pillars of my arms should be held upright with only enough tension to keep my hands up. Strength is applied only when needed in order to defend or to make an offensive action. The fists aren't clenched until just before the punch lands.

A good jab really POPS! into the target. The elbow remains down and does not fly out (and therefore signal your intention) before the punch begins. When you land it clean you can feel it — like hitting a sweetspot. Al has me breathe out in short, spitting wheezes with each jab. WHAP! WHAP! WHAP! This is fun!

We practice that for a bit and then he has me move and jab at the same time. Going back and forth *and* bobbing *and* jabbing is a real exercise in rhythm. I do pretty well, although I'm tempted to break out into full boogie mode because it really does seem like a dance now. When I start to move my hands to the beat in my mind Al tells me to keep my hands up and still.

After happily smacking his targeted hands for about a minute or so, Al shows me how to defend against the jab. As the jab comes, you catch the fist with the palm of your leading glove as your glove rests on your forehead. Catching the jab away from your face won't stop the punch as both your opponent's jabbing fist and your catching glove will come crashing into your kisser. It's also important that your catching glove rests upon your forehead and not your nose. As you catch the jab in this manner, you pivot your rear foot, plant yourself on the ball of your foot and remain firm. You take jabs as aggressively as you give them.

Again this is a rhythm, timing thing (and if you're indeed clumsy you should not be boxing until you can dance along with Soul Train). Al takes a few swings with his padded palms and I catch them as instructed. After a while it dawns on me that I'm actually being punched *at*. This is a revelation of sorts because all lesson long I've been the aggressor. It has slipped my mind that someone is eventually gonna take a swing at me.

So I start to flinch. This is a real drawback in boxing. I start to laugh, thinking about fighting somebody with eyes closed and Al says yeah, you gotta keep them open. He says when he was learning as a kid that he'd walk around chopping himself between the eyes in order to develop control. One of his friends was so good he could poke himself in the eye without blinking.

That's about it for day one. We decide to meet at ten on Tuesday and Thursday mornings.

WHALING   7-31-97: Lesson #3

I'm feeling somewhat distracted this morning due to some business snafus and hardly in the mood for much of anything fun (a strange but common enough state of self-flagellation). I feel worse when Al asks me if I've practiced and I say no. But we go over things and it gets better.

It gets a whole lot better when we go over to the heavy bag and I do three-minute punching drills. Al has me jab, work with a straight right and combinations thereof. I finally start to whale with the one-two and I mean WHALE. I beat the bag until my arms hurt and the sweat pours on the floor. Hitting it properly yields a very sweet POP! and oddly enough the bag doesn't sway as much as you might think. It's when you push after the punch that the bag starts to twist and turn. The trick is to snap it out and pull back in immediately. I do great for a minute or so, but by the end of the drill I'm pretty tired and start to lunge my punches and drop my arms. This is hard work!

The Left Hook

The next new punch to learn is the left hook. For some reason I was thinking it would be a roundhouse thing that swings in a big looping (and hook-like) fashion, but it isn't an arm punch at all. This is a punch powered by shoulder, torso and legs, usually after

> I'm feeling totally drained of the heeby-jeebs I came in with. Beat the bag, beat the blues. Yeah!

throwing a right hand. With your weight transferring from right to left leg, bend your left arm at the elbow, lift the elbow up and out (here's where they get the hook) and pivot everything around. I'm thinking it's sorta like a swinging gate. The gate is your left arm, shoulder and torso — all in a single piece — pivoting with the left foot. It's very difficult to coordinate and after a few attempts, Al tells me to give it a rest. He says it's the most difficult punch to learn and you can't expect to get it down right away.

He does show me the drill to use with the hook and it's a drill I've seen boxers do a lot. Throw the straight right, then throw the hook. Right-left, right-left, right-left and so on. It's a powerful combination of punches that I've seen over and over again during boxing matches, yet until now, never really understood.

We close the session by going over all the punches I can throw in reps of ten: jabs, straight rights and one-two combinations. Walking out of the gym and to the van I'm feeling totally drained of the heeby-jeebs I came in with. Beat the bag, beat the blues. Yeah!

EATING PUNCHES 8-7-97: Lesson #5

I wrap my own hands today. As usual I start with some stepping drills in all four directions. Starting with three each way, then two, then one. I jab with each step and finish with a right.

The problems I have remembering steps and form (along with everything else!) are continuous and amusing, at least to me. Al is always ready to laugh, too, but I don't think he sees my boxing lessons from the same point of whimsey that I often do (Hey! Lookit me! I'm learning how to box!) Sometimes I have to laugh out loud. I guess I'm simply enjoying myself.

We put on my gloves and Al puts on his hand pads to work on a new sequence where I throw jab, right, hook and then duck under his own punches. Ducking is a matter of squatting straight down under the punch and sliding towards the side your opponent is throwing from. This is called a **V** slide. This is my first drill where offense and defense are combined and it's thrilling when we do a few sequences at a brisk pace and the punches whiz over my head (Wow, I'm ducking punches!) A couple land on top of my head but Al is swinging so lightly it's no big deal. The idea is to duck in close to your opponent so he cannot land forceful blows.

In front of the mirror, Al has me do right-left, left-right slides (straight right hand-left hook-left slide, then left hook-straight right hand-right slide) one after the other until the sweat starts to rain from my face. It's really hard to do and I get frustrated. My right's OK but my left hook looks awful. I stop and start until Al says I won't get it right away anyway so just DO IT. As I complete a few dozen it gets better but not much. Al demonstrates along with me (he's always moving) and makes it look easy.

Going over to the bag we work on an impossible drill where I gotta step into each punch in a left-right-left combo. It's ugly. I'm used to punching without stepping and as odd as it sounds adding the step throws everything off. I try and try but it feels so awkward and sloppy. It's the first drill that Al's shown me that I just can't do ... yet.

As if that isn't enough (there are no breaks in Al's Academy of Boxing — instruction, patter and drilling is ceaseless, overlapping and just short of overload. The guy is a good coach and makes every lesson a dynamic blur). Al has me step up on a stationary platform to work on the right-left thing (again) so that I can concentrate on keeping my feet still. Now I'm really sweating (there's actually a stream of sweat *jumping* off my forehead) and the left hook looks only slightly better after swinging it along with the right 50 times. But Al says no worries ... it'll come ... I was worse at that stage ... etc.

We finish with that skipping-over-the-rope thing and whew! ... what a workout!

TIED UP 8-14-97: Lesson #7

I thought I'd try to pace myself today since I wore myself out during the first few minutes of my last session. After wrapping up, I shadowbox a bit and Al has me work on long and short rhythms. Long is

> He ties my right arm with a spare wrap and makes me jab until my left deltoid burns.

a loose, up and back thing (like Muhammad Ali). Short is a quicker, side-to-side thing where you move your head and shoulders a lot (like Joe Frazer or Mike Tyson in his prime). It's not so difficult, really, and I pick it up OK ... for now.

Then we move over to the heavy bag for some drills with the combinations. Later Al puts on his mitts and has me work various combos with him hitting back (lightly) so I have to think about defense as well as offensive technique. This is fun. And putting it all together, especially with the more involved exchanges, is very challenging. For example: I throw a one-two, after which he throws a hook which I duck, after which I throw a right, after which he throws a right hook which I block, after which I immediately react with a hook. The reaction punch is your fastest offensive threat. It's basically punching into an opponent's unguarded area as he punches.

These exchanges are exhilarating but after a while I forget what to do and literally spaz out — covering my head, backing away, etc. Al just laughs and says it's natural to bail like that and it takes some time not to give in to the instinct. He goes on to say that it's important to learn how to commit to your punches, especially when you see the other guy start to unload on you. It's better to finish your action than it is to give up and cover, since your punch can land or at least defuse your opponent's punch.

We go back to the bag to fine tune my punching technique. We start with the jab which I throw too low at first. Since I have a tendency to drop my right during the jab, Al makes me hold a mitt in my right arm pit to keep my arm close to my body. Not quite satisfied with that, he ties my right arm with a spare wrap and makes me jab until my left deltoid burns. As I toil away he tells me this sordid tale about his early training when his coach tied him up and made him jab that way for two months. After an endless three minutes he unties me and makes me do one-twos in yet another vicious three-minute drill, which I'm convinced is closer to four (Al is a tough taskmaster and is not above stretching out the pain).

Wobbly by now, I go over to the smaller punching bag and he teaches me the trick to drilling away at the bladder. It's all in the timing and striking technique he tells me, and without looking makes the thing rattle along like it's wired to a machine. A light, quick hitting action makes the thing go pop-pop-pop. It's the quick recovery after the hit that matters most and hitting the thing as it comes towards you. After you get going, it's in the timing. I try it slowhand and it works ... for a little while anyway.

Finally, Al has me do these skipping/hopping things over a rope on the floor and I finish with five minutes of skipping rope which amounts to about 200 skips. It's another workout, brother. I'm drenched and drained. These days I bring a towel and a dry shirt. I haven't slaved away like this since high-school wrestling.

Another surprise tidbit (and there seem to be lots of surprises in this boxing stuff): under responsible supervision, it takes about six months of training to get into the ring for three rounds of sparring. You gotta know your stuff before they'll let you fight.

LIKE GOLF 8-21-97: Lesson #8

My hands ache because I've been tying them up too tight with the wraps. Al wraps my hands today and his wraps are much looser than mine.

We do some shadowboxing, specifically working on the hook. He has me step into the hook — marching across the room leading with my right foot and punching with the left step. It's a good exercise and it gets me to swing the body into the punch. I'm supposed to feel it in my stomach!

Working with the hand pads, Al has me throw various punches and combinations. First jabs ... again and again and again. Then double jabs ... again and again and again. Then one-twos. Then one-twos with a hook. Then one-twos with a hook and a right. It's difficult to pivot off each foot correctly and maintain proper balance throughout. Man, it's hard to put it all together! Just like the dog-gone golf swing!

When Al starts slapping me around for real I start learning much faster (imagine that!)

Al starts throwing punches to make the mix even more interesting. I throw a left and a right, duck his left, slide back to my left foot and throw a right ... and then sometimes a hook. Then he has me throw some counter-punches. Again, the exciting interplay of actually working off someone.

We work some new defenses in front of the mirror where I protect head and body — left side, right side — in a very rhythmic fashion that I get and forget, get and forget — just like everything else at first (such a precise and particular pursuit, this boxing). Of course, when Al starts slapping me around for real I start learning much faster (imagine that!) and yes, it's a very good idea to keep even these easy slaps from landing. The trick is to keep hands and head properly positioned from the get-go so that any defensive maneuvering takes only a sleight of hand and a minor flex in the knees.

We go over to Mr. Heavy Bag and Al shows me how to work on right and left power punch combos. It's all timing, where you hit the bag during the particular moment it swings toward the punch. It's new, it's difficult and I hurt my hand. So we stop and Al has me skip rope bouncing on two feet, my right foot and finally my left. Since I'm tired the skipping goes rather poorly, but I muddle through and Al (ever the UPBEAT coach) says, "You did great today! See you next week!"

BUT YOU'RE KILLING ME! 8-26-97: Lesson #8

After a lumbering warm-up in front of Mr. Coach and the mirror (my moves are so clunky ... just can't dance) Al puts on the slap mitts and we work on offense and defense. I throw punches, he returns fire, I block and counterpunch. He really mixes it up so it's alotta fun. The trick is to have confidence in your basic defense and punch so that when your opponent strikes back (as he will!) you don't flinch and withdraw. You gotta get to the point where you don't care what he's throwing because you've got your own game plan to worry about.

If you keep thinking about what's coming, it's gonna be all over!

Of course, easier said than done. It's only natural to flinch and hesitate when you're under attack. Al catches me off guard plenty with his change ups, but that's cool. I get better and pretty soon I'm doing pretty darn good — smacking the mitts, fending off the blows and hitting back with the right counterpunches. It's great fun and I'm pleased that my punches are snapping on the sweetspot and that I'm in balance most of the time. It's so easy to lose that center of gravity when you're whaling away.

During the lesson some older fellow comes into the room to hit the overhead bag. He hits away and rests, hits away and rests, and when he rests, he looks at me and mumbles encouragement that I can't really hear, but it's nice that he's rooting just the same. And I'm pleased with myself for drilling so well with an audience (of sorts). We work on the left hook a bit and Al reminds me of the stepping drill to use with the hook in order to force myself to *step* into the punch. I gotta remember to incorporate that into my home workout.

At one point he has me land a series of rights and lefts upon his mitts which he places high overhead. This reaching and punching is a mean workout. I feel it in my stomach, arms and back. We go in series of ten for about ten times and it's all I can do to finish the drill. I'm so bushed that I'm thinking the lesson is over, but then Al points to the heavy bag (this guy's gonna kill me!).

Al wants me to go two rounds on the bag. First as a lightweight (with technique and quick footwork), then as a BIG PUNCHING heavyweight. Well, rounds are three minutes long, but since I'm so tired they seem eternal. I start off OK but soon my arms drag and loose their speed. I drop my guard, throw off the wrong foot, pant, wheeze and sweat ... sweat ... sweat. After the three minutes, I rest for one teeny minute before I stumble through round two and I mean stumble. Afterward, I ask Al if my form was as bad as it felt. He just says yep.

As I take off gloves and wraps I ask about boxing some*body* as opposed to some *bag*. He says we'll start into that slowly when I can throw the punches, defend myself and last three rounds. He

> **I was wondering about getting hit on some level (hey, natural enough) and his easy-does-it philosophy sounds good to me.**

likes to start guys off, say, with jabs only. Or one guy throws while the other guy defends. It's an incremental type of thing. He teaches his JV football team the same way. The kids have never really hit anybody or been hit before so there's a gradual introduction to blocking and tackling. Al says he isn't from the Boxing School of Hard Knocks and for that I'm relieved. I guess I was wondering about getting hit on some level (hey, natural enough) and his easy-does-it philosophy sounds good to me. I can only imagine what getting hit, time after time, is like. I guess it's the training that sees you through. At any rate, the little talk was a good one. It gave me confidence in the plan and the coach.

You know, I did well today. I felt it and Al saw it, too. Especially during the action/reaction part of the lesson. Al says that is a watershed in the boxing education — being able to ride with the offensive/defensive flow and flurry. Awright!

GOT THAT? 8-28-97: Lesson #9

I mix it up with shadowboxing at first — rights, lefts and some defensive moves, etc. It doesn't look very good. Like I'm still a little uncoordinated.

Al teaches me the uppercut, which is something like a hook since you use legs and torso to drive the punch. The direction of the punch is up after you tilt your body to the side of the punching arm.

Al springs a 12-punch combo on me today that I sorta get, but I mean really — I'm supposed to remember 12 punches and their sequential order? Right! What I execute looks OK, though, and when I just let myself go with it, I do remember most of it.

Then he shows me this drill where you throw straight rights and lefts followed by left hooks and right uppercuts. He says this is really hard and that he'd be impressed if I got it right away. The drill is difficult, but after a few tries I start to get it in a ragged fashion. I'm elated because it's the first time I've been able to get one of these high coordination drills right off. What makes it hard is the constant, nonstop change of direction that each punch requires. All the different angles make this combination very effective in a fight. Your opponent can't anticipate so many attacking angles coming at him so quickly.

After this resounding success, Al puts on the slap mitts and has me go over some of the reaction punches. He hits me on one side and I immediately throw the hand on that side in a counteraction followed by another left or right. I'm all screwed up with this drill after a while although it's fun acting and reacting with another boxer. Sometimes Al feints his slaps and we both laugh when I come undone in false anticipation. The idea is to follow through with your intentions (BAD INTENTIONS, he calls them) no matter what the other guy does.

We finish up with the heavy bag. I practice throwing three straight hands while stepping into the bag. It's not easy coordinating the small shuffling steps with each punch and after a few stumbling efforts Al has me skip some rope and we call it a day.

REAL MEN JUMP ROPE 9-4-97: Lesson #10

I show up already wrapped and Al laughs. He says *this guy's serious!* I say it's important to be ready when you're walking the *mean streets of La Jolla.*

I missed Tuesday's lesson and it shows. Shadowboxing is a joke. I try to get into a rhythm and it looks like I've just shot up elephant tranquilizers. Al just stands there speechless.

We work on defense and counterpunching, which I enjoy because I get to play off Al's moves (I spend so much of my time practicing with a bag or a reflection of myself that it's a pure joy to interact!) My reflexes aren't all that sharp though. What I was doing so well last week escapes me today. Al, always the savvy coach, tries different gears to keep the thing going (it always goes and goes ... no problem there) and it's a good exercise all the same. I go a few

About this jumping rope. It ain't easy or pansy.

rounds with the heavy bag until my jab lands like a slap. This goes better (I *have* been hitting the bag a lot at home) and my left hook is coming along. It's alotta work and the last punches are like digging a damn ditch (Al: *Come on! Thirty seconds more!*) but it finally ends in a sweat-soaked flourish ... and then it's time to jump rope.

About this jumping rope. It ain't easy or pansy, let me tell you. Not the way EL COACHO likes to see it done, anyway. Try ten reps skipping with both feet, next ten with one, then ten with the other. Repeat in a descending count (reps of 9, 8, 7, etc.) until you're skipping two feet, right foot and finally left in sequence. Hey, it was hard enough just getting to 100 jumping with both feet last week. Going to a single leg is murder! I've been working on this on my patio and have gotten to the point where I only have to stop and start again two or three times.

But after an hour-long lesson with Al (and that's a FULL hour, baby) jumping rope is like lifting potato sacks. By the time I'm through I'm woozy, wobbly and dripping wet on my feet. And feeling absolutely wonderful!

ART & BLOODY NOSES 10-16-97: Lesson #20

I go six rounds on the pillar, struggling with the last round or two. Al puts on his mitts and we work on punches and counters. I perk up for this — it's so much fun. I do fairly well, not hesitating or getting baffled like I sometimes do when Al goes offensive. My balance is better, too. I still drop my right and square off too much (getting out of the boxer's stance during inside fighting), among other things, but all-in-all not bad.

My form is OK before fatigue sets in. Punches are strong and snappy. My footwork has a touch of grace and spunk to it. When I start to get tired the crispness goes. I push my punches and plod. My jab is especially affected. It lands with a slap instead of a POP! and man does my left shoulder ache!

We work on slips and ducks. I'm really weak with my boxing rhythm and my head movement. I feel like such a plodder. I should be working on this at home. I go another round on the pillar and finish jumping rope.

Al and I discuss the differences between Asian martial arts instruction and boxing. Seems boxing just doesn't have the same sizzle as the other. One is perceived as some kind of arty workout while boxing is just bloody noses or something. Al says the martial arts are more structured for learning, having so many stages and the like (white belt, brown belt, black belt, etc.). Boxing instruction gets right down to it without the years of instruction and the spiritual shadings.

This leads to the questions: Why not include similar stages to boxing instruction? Why not define levels of expertise in the manner of the martial arts? And why not emphasize the mental as well as the physical challenges of boxing as well (as they do in the other combat disciplines). I've only had 20 lessons, but I know this much: boxing is much more than slugging it out! It's a sport that rewards grace, coordination and strategic thinking (hey, that sounds like fencing).

I know I'm a little green at this stuff to be spouting off, but what is it with the meager perception of boxing (especially among middle-class Americans) and why are the other forms of hand-to-hand combat held in such esteem? Why do mothers send their tykes to karate class without blinking an eye, but would never dream of having little Tommy (or Susie) attend a boxing class?

PUMPED! SPARRING AT LAST 10-21-97: Lesson #21

After some rounds on Mr. Pillar Punch (a freestanding heavy bag), Al puts on the mitts and we go over the jab. First without Al throwing return fire, then with. It gets real interesting when he throws jabs straight into my face as I throw my own. Of course, I must continue with my action while catching his jab with my right hand.

Then a surprise. Al puts on a pair of gloves and away we go! *Just throw slow jabs* he says — *70% or so.* Well, this is exciting. At last! Toe to toe. Boxing for real! At first I hesitate to hit *him* because inflicting pain on others is not a natural part of my personality (is it anybody's?). But I keep telling him it's OK to hit *me* (I think) because I don't want him holding back too much. *I'm not a piece of glass,* I say.

Quit running around, Al says. You're going spastic.

It's so DIFFERENT with a real person. Who LOOKS at you. Who BOXES with you. Right there in FRONT of you. Who SWINGS at you. Who's COMING AFTER YOU.

We dance around too much cause I'm goin' nuts with my feet for some reason. Al stops to tell me to quit running around (you're going spastic, he says.) We continue and he has no problem bouncing his jabs off my forehead (we're supposed to be aiming at each other there). I finally get into it and toss a few soggy left hands into his gloves. I actually hit him once or twice, but not very well or very hard. He's actually very difficult to target as he bobs and weaves all over the place. I don't move much and tend to charge into his hitting zone and stay there. I'm a punching bag, but he knows how to pull his punches so there is no damage, although he bonks me in the nose once — a minor wake-up call.

I get tired because of the previous workout and the fighting makes me very tense. Al tells me to breathe (I don't even breathe I'm so jacked up!). I have to stop to rest once, but when he asks if I've had enough, I say HECK NO! and we go another round. When we finish Al tells me that I did very well. *You didn't back off,* he says. *You've got what it takes mentally.*

Naturally, this makes me feel like a million bucks, although I feel my performance was sorta limp wristed. My punches were so weak! Al says I just don't know how to throw into live action yet. *It's really different, but you'll get it,* he says. *It looks like you've got your first ding, too.*

Sure enough, that little tap on the nose gave me a slight bruise. My first scar! And I didn't feel a thing. Can I take a punch or what?

Later we talk about other damage he's dealt his students (by mistake, of course). Once his dentist and he did a little sparring, and Al broke the guy's rib. Apparently only 12 pounds of pressure can crack a rib. The dentist survived, but I have a feeling that it's Al who gets worked sometimes. After all, he's the one catching all the practice punches with his mitts. He's the one pulling his punches. Not the students. We get into it and it's bombs away because we forget everything in the melee.

Did I say that this was a lot of fun? I'm ordering headgear and sparring gloves this week because the gloves we used today are really for bags only. Sparring gloves are more heavily padded.

HEY BIG BOY 10-30-97: Lesson #24

As before, three or four rounds on the pillar, then the mitts. My jab is better today. Stronger. Keeping the elbows in, throwing straight out from the chin and recovering sharply. Did OK with the mitts. Reaction time much better than last session.

Had something of an audience today. One of the people who works at the gym came into our room a coupla times to fetch equipment. Although she was pretty much dashing in and out, she made a very generous comment about my performance on her second trip. *You're really good! Did you know that?* Al and I are working the mitts and we both just stop dead. *Well you are,* she says. *Does he tell you that? Come on, Alan, tell him he's good.*

Of course, this sounds real good to me because I've been thinking how bad I am (dropping my right, confusing punches, etc.) and though Al has never said I stink, he has never said I'm very good either. So to hear a compliment of this magnitude is not only encouraging, it's downright stunning.

Al is taken aback and I can tell he wants to ignore her interference, but since that would be impossible (she's waiting for an answer), he says *all right, you're good* and she prances out of the room. I laugh and say *she wrecked the entire coaching scenario, didn't she?* Al says *yeah, and now I've got to deal with your big head.* It's all very amusing because after all, what does she know. But damn I feel good!

Looking good! she says. I must be stylin!

Another person comes in to watch, and although he doesn't insist that Al compliment my performance, I feel I'm finishing our session strongly and probably looking OK out there. Then I think that Al

> You're really good, she says. Does he tell you that? Come on, Alan, tell him he's good.

must be pleased, too, since he's the coach and the man responsible for any progress I've made.

Later That Day: Oh, What a Pretty Groin Protector!

The rest of my sparring gear arrives: groin protector, mouthpiece and gloves. My wife is the first to wear the stuff, however, as she decides to be a boxer at the office Halloween party. The groin apparatus with the big red, shiney cup is especially becoming on her.

WW II, CLEAVAGE & NUTS

11-20-97: Lesson #29

As I tape up for class, the older gent comes in to swing at the overhead bag. He's the same guy who a few weeks ago used to hit the bag, hang out, watch and make funny comments.

We talk a bit and he says he used to box in college and the Navy. He says he's the *old man* around here. I'm thinking he's 60-something, but he's gonna be 75 this week. I say you don't *look* 75 and mean it. He laughs and says yeah, I'd look 50 if I lost some weight and I believe it. He says women come on to him until they find out how old he is. Then he blurts *hell, I was in World War Two!* This stops us both because (wow!) that is rather extraordinary and a little surprising ... to both of us.

Al comes in and we charge through another session. After the pillar pounding, we go to the mitts and work on footwork, slips and the 1-2-3 combo.

What's different today is throwing punches while moving my feet. As we move back in a straight line, Al throws a right and then a left after my 1-2-3 that I must try to slip. Up until now I've been stationary. This is difficult, moving the left foot with the left and the right foot with the right. I have a tendency to overstep and square off. But after a while I get the hang of it. Sorta.

In the middle of all this I see a pretty lady with gorgeous breasts choosing her weights on the other side of the glass partition. Since she's bending down and showing a ton of cleavage, it's all I can do to focus on Al and his mitts. He turns me the other way (so he can look) and makes me work. Did I say he was a tough, no-nonsense coach? Rocky never had distractions like this in his gym.

I finish with some rope work and do spectacularly well until I hit my nuts with the handle (I don't know how this happens). As I sink to my knees, Al cracks up and admits that this has been an entertaining lesson for sure.

Before class I had the opportunity to explain the lure of boxing to a young lady who was curious about this, my latest project. Among other things, I said it's great for women, too. But she just crinkled her nose.

I said *well, I bet you think karate is OK, right?* And she said *well, yeah, I'd consider trying that.* I said *that's because Hollywood makes the martial arts seem more appealing, and more sexy, but boxing is every bit as athletic and graceful* — that *professional boxing has ruined the public's perception of boxing in general,* and so on.

I don't know if she bought any of my spiel but she listened without any further crinkling of her nose, and it gave me some practice with my BOX FOR FUN AND FITNESS line. One thing is for sure: boxing definitely needs some spin doctoring other than from Mr. Don King. The public's perception of boxing is pretty dismal and a lot of it is just plain wrong.

Somebody should write a book!

THIS'LL SHUT HIM UP 12-9-97: Lesson #33

Not a bad one today. Inside fighting. Working head and shoulders together with brisk bunches of punches. My rhythm is better. We work the pillar first, then Al puts on a glove and throws jabs, which I must slip. I do surprisingly well (practicing at home helps) and then it happens again — a woman comes in, looks at me and exclaims *you're good!* As before, we're both stunned. And again, although I'm grateful, Al is mildly irritated with the distraction.

That sounds great. You punch my head and I punch your mitt.

She says something to Al as I rest. After she leaves, Al tells me that he put on a boxing clinic for her son's 14th birthday over the weekend. One of the kids had a big mouth so Al had him spar with someone who clocked him. I ask if he set it up that way and he laughs and says *yeah, sorta. He was a real pain. A spoiled La Jolla rich kid.* I start laughing so loud everyone on the other side of the glass looks over. Apparently the woman was all right with the scuffle as she was all smiles when she came in. I'm thinking *Alan, you're a sly dog.* As well as *brother, don't ever mess with Coach!*

After the slipping exercise, I go a round or two on the mitts and work on the cutting off techniques we went over a few weeks ago. This entails moving to the right or left with your opponent as he moves, fencing him in with right or left hooks to the body. As I'm very tired by now, it's all I can do to remember which foot to lead with when I move laterally.

We wrap it up and Al is pleased. *You slip better than me. You've really improved.* I say thanks, I've been practicing footwork at home. He says we'll be incorporating some contact into each lesson from now on. I'm stoked. The closer we get to combat the better. It's the only way to really learn some of this stuff and with contact you learn fast!

GO AHEAD, HIT ME 12-16-97: Lesson #34

Some work on the pillar then something a little different. Al hangs a rope from the ceiling with a large knot dangling on one end. He swings it and shows me how to avoid the knot by slipping. The knot is about head high and the trick is to move your head just enough to let the knot slip by. Actually, we went over this eons ago (man, it's been five months since I started!) but now it makes more sense as I'm beginning to work head and shoulder movements into my routine, which includes semi-sparring with Al (where I'd better move my noggin or else!).

I'm awkward at first but it starts to gel. I stare at the mirror as the knot swings in order to avoid its return sweep. It's a good drill. Makes you develop some rhythm in a fashion you'd never have to use otherwise (after all, you never bob like this in any other pursuit).

Then Al has me put on headgear and insert mouthpiece. He slips on a glove and a focus mitt. He throws jabs and left hooks that I must slip or block. I throw at his mitt (he asks me to remember not to punch his face ... I think *oh that's just great ... you punch my head and I punch your hand ... thank you very much!*) with jabs and an occasional right hand.

The first round of this drill is clumsy as I get used to getting hit, defending myself and throwing punches all at the same time. It's pretty confusing but very, very exciting. I automatically start dancing around like a fool, but this ain't where it's at. The thing you want to do is to control and conserve your movements. All the running around just tires me out. As we go on, I try to use my feet less and my head movements more. This is tough because I get tagged every now and then.

Although Al is punching lightly (for him) his blows are still something I'd rather avoid. My slipping and blocking improve dramatically (no kidding!) as we continue to spar another round or two. By the fourth round I'm into it. This is it. I'm doing OK and even Al says so.

I'm not really shy of being hit, it's the confusion that sometimes occurs that bothers me most. Losing control, taking my eyes off Al during a punch, thinking too much, getting all jumpy, etc. Actually, I laugh every time I really get nailed. I ask Al if that's a good sign and he says *yeah, I guess* ... and he starts laughing, too.

What can I say? Just having a wonderful time eating leather.

I hope this contact stuff gets more and more airplay. It's a great way to learn and beats hell out of all the drills. Heck, I've been drilling since July!

STUNG BUT GAME 12-18-97: Lesson #35

After some work on the pillar we spar as before: I throw jabs and

> **That punch has lost me a few clients, he says. You definitely have the right attitude.**

rights at a mitt and Al throws jabs and lefts at my face. I don't slip very well today. Actually, I forget the fundamentals and do this pawing and reaching that gets me punched time and time again. I'm mad at myself for performing so miserably: dancing around, sticking my face in his striking zone, little head movement, leaning back, slapping my punches, hesitating, letting Al dictate the action, you name it. I say *after 34 lessons I'm not showing a thing!*

Al says I did better last session, but at least I realize all my mistakes and that's what matters at this point. After all, this is only the third or fourth sparring session. Actually Alan is happy enough with my improvement overall and particularly impressed with the way I took a left hook to the body today.

This punch stung and for about a long second really shut me down. I just sorta went *Oh!* when it landed and we both knew I needed a short break to come back to life. I got back on it, however, fairly quickly. The thing is, hurties are gonna happen and you simply gotta learn to suck it up if you wanna spar. Al says that punch separates those who continue and those who quit. I remembered his story about the dentist with the broken rib. *That punch has lost me a few clients* he says. *You definitely have the right attitude.*

So I'm coming back. I know I can spar better than I did today, and outside of the occasional incoming bomb, it's absolutely exhilarating.

ATTA BOY! 12-23-97: Lesson #36

The rib hurt like hell for a day or two. I thought it was busted, but yesterday I did a full workout without repercussion, so here we go.

On the pillar Al had me work on lighter, quicker jabs. He says most of my jabs are loaded and that I ought to mix it up with faster, snappier ones, too. Again the emphasis on mixing it up — presenting a less predictable game plan. Also tips for my hook — the need to snap it back. Al says the hook is looking all right, otherwise. The most important observation today: thinking defense with my punches. That is, getting back to guard quickly and properly after each punch. This instills confidence to throw more as I get better and better at recovery (knowing I should be able to throw and recover before a counterpunch). Working on this double concept actually improves my form today. In particular, I feel my forearms are arranging themselves better throughout my work with combinations.

The old man is in our room today. He bangs away at the overhead for a while and watches Al and me work. He makes his comments here and there and it's OK. When we spar he has a lot more to say... *keep the hands up ... watch out for the left hook ... hey, Alan's reach is longer than yours ... use the right hand ...* that sort of thing. His heart's exactly in the right place and he wants to see improvement.

My performance is 100% better says Al. I think it's better than last Tuesday's, for sure. I slipped some punches very cleanly and threw more punches, too. I reached less and stopped doing that pawing and leaning back business. I got caught with my hands too far in front once or twice and left myself open for the left hook. I did my best work when I kept the basic stance intact and made the side-to-side moves. Al says I need to think offensively along with the slips, though. Execute the defense and retaliate at once. Don't think about it.

Of course, I'm hitting a punch mitt and Al's punching at my face so the intimidation factor rears its ugly head now and then. I mean, what's he got to be afraid of? But I work through it and by the third round of sparring my biggest problem is energy.

We talk a little about getting hit. It's definitely a new dimension after dancing with the bag for so long. I say the head shots so far don't bother me much, but the body shot I took last week sure did.

I'm happy. The rib's getting better and my sparring improved. I'm at the point where I can pretty much see my errors and know what I need to work on in my training. I can see (or at least imagine) the beauty of really getting it right, and I'm looking forward to seeing some of these bits of offensive and defensive skills come together.

> **I was told that your top yogettes would be sparring with me today.**

FOUR HOOKS TO THE HEAD

12-30-97: Lesson #37

After the long break I feel a little less sharp but not too much. Four rounds on the pillar, four rounds of semi-sparring and one more round on the pillar. Nine rounds is working OUT!

I work on quick jabs. During the sparring I try to keep my hands back and around my cheeks but still get caught off guard at times. Actually I get hooked four times because my hands are out front — pawing again! My actions are just too predictable. And not enough head movement, especially after I throw. I have the tendency to stop and keep my face in Al's striking zone. Not good.

The positive is that I know I'm screwing up as soon as I screw up. I'm becoming that aware of the action. I'm not throwing enough punches, I'm not throwing off my slips enough (offense off the defense) and I'm still dancing a bit too much. All this I know and actually make some improvements from round to round.

The fourth round is my best. I request the fourth round (Al planned to go three) because I know I can improve, I have the energy and it's too much fun to stop. Although I do alotta stuff better, I get hit with two hooks in this round. I guess ya gotta take some to give some.

They don't hurt much. In fact, we joke about the shots when they land. In between punches I say *he* (referring to myself) *ain't much to look at but he's got a great sense of humor* and such things, which crack Al and me up (but maybe you had to be there).

I finish on the pillar. It's a long three minutes because I'm bushed. Afterward we talk a little about exhaustion — how I used to wobble out of here after a lesson. Al says he used to be brain-drained after sparring — so tired he couldn't even think. I laugh and say how great that is — anything to leave modern life behind. Al says you get punched enough and you leave everything behind for good. I say perhaps I'll stop short of that, although it seems that some punch drunk guys sure *look* pretty happy. Laughs.

YOGETTES TURN UP THE HEAT 1-2-98: Lesson #38

No sparring today due to a conflicting yoga class in our boxing studio. The yoga instructor, a high-toned dame, says to Alan *but dahling, our class meets at this time, remembahhh?* Well, I can't pass this up. I say something like *but I was told that your top yogettes would be sparring with me today.* Of course, this goes over like a lead balloon (she barely glances in my direction) which makes it all the more funny (to me anyway).

As I laugh all by myself, Al diplomatically points out that she's actually early and that we'll be outta there in 30 minutes. She's good natured enough not to sniff too loud, picks up her pad and bottled water and whisks her way to the other side of the room where she instructs one of her students while I sweat and pound on the pillar (this is such a contrast -- the mellow yoga versus the thumping boxing lesson). This arrangement works well enough (it's a big room), however the yoga folks turn the damn heat on, and in no time I'm burning up.

We zip through the basic stuff and head onto the main floor where Al shows me some special exercises to do with a stretch cord. The latter is simply stretchable tubing with a handle at each end. Al attaches one of the handles to an exercise machine in front of a mirror and has me practice my jab and my right while holding the other handle. As usual, I go three minutes on each punch. It really burns after a minute or so and the last minute is tough. I complain a little but Al just does one of his Drill Sergeant routines *(Come on! Let's do it!)* in front of all the old men and ladies that frequent this place at this hour and shames me into finishing the repetition.

After that he has me sit down and do these twist-at-the-waist things catching and throwing a six-pound medicine ball. It's not difficult but after about 30 on each side, I'm tired. I ask him if doing all this stuff with the stretch cord and the medicine ball after 30 minutes on the heavy bag constitutes a pretty stiff workout and Al says *no, it's pretty low end. We used to use a cord on each hand at the same time and toss a twelve-pound ball.*

> ## It's ridiculous – here I am boxing and getting so mad I wanna hit something – but I can't.

BUT THAT CAN'T BE ME!

1-6-98: Lesson #39

Al video tapes our session today from bag to sparring. Quick looks after each round reveal ugliness ...*God, I'm slow! Look how I drop my hands! I'm a bum! ... cheez ...*

Sparring is fun. I dance while Al stalks. We go four rounds. By the third he's throwing his padded right hand as well as the gloved left. I slip a few ... it's not a bad showing. But every now and then I let up and my confidence goes. I start watching his hands and hesitate to throw. I shake my head and force myself to hang in there.

Later in the Day ...

Time to really look at the tapes ...

After first review:

1) I need to pick up the pace, especially with the jab.
2) My hands are too low. They drop when I get tired.
3) I'm still too predictable. I need to work on mixing up my movements — offensive and defensive.
4) I need to throw more punches during the sparring work — especially the right hand.
5) I still paw and lean back a little.
6) In general I need to work on the side-to-side stuff and develop quicker movements.
7) My left hook has a wind-up — needs to be thrown from guard.
8) My one-twos need a stronger, more full jab.

HEAVY DUES   1-13-98: Lesson #42

After four rounds on the pillar, Al puts on two gloves and inserts a mouthpiece. We're gonna spar.

I ask *where's your headgear* and he says *I don't need it.* Well, OK.

Like the first time, it takes me a minute or two just to stop from racing around. I get so tense! I try to come in with some jabs, but it seems like Al's always 10 feet away. He, however, has no problem landing anything he wants. This goes on for one round. I slip some and maybe graze him with a punch or two, but I'm totally out-classed. It's pretty much the same for the next round. I try ducking in with body shots, but again I'm too far away. At one point I charge in and get walloped good with jabs and hooks. I glance over to the viewing window and there's a guy looking in. I'm thinking great, I'm looking like a bum out here and I've got an audience.

Later on I lose it. I guess (it's all guessing when you're in the middle of all this — so much intensity) it happens when I try to come in and get slapped around for the umpteenth time. I start yelling through my mouthpiece and stamping my feet. It's so ridiculous. I mean, here I am boxing and getting so mad I wanna hit something — but I can't. So I throw this fit, which immediately makes me feel like the biggest fool on earth. Al says *Cool it! Get back to it!* Things like that. I'm embarrassed and say I'm not mad at you. I'm mad at myself (true). And we get back to it.

For maybe 30 seconds into the last round I show some poise, but then all I can see are Al's gloves ready to swat my face. It takes every fiber of my training to carry on. Oh man, what a dreadful experi-ence. Yeah, I get rocked a little, but it isn't that so much as not being able to land anything or even dodge much. I feel like I'm throwing it all away out there. And blowing my cool like that is a thousand times more painful than any punch I'm taking.

Al says I didn't do as bad as I think. He explains the facts of our bout: I'm matched with someone better than me (no kidding!), I need to gain ground incrementally during such a match-up. Get in closer inch by inch until I can finally reach. This may mean getting hit but there it is. Charging in makes everything so much worse. I can't be tossing aside all I've learned like that and expect anything good to come of it. He says not to worry about getting upset. I'm only frus-trated and that's natural. Everyone has to go through it. I need to be patient and use my training. He laughs and says *you're paying your dues!* Then he has me go another two rounds on the pillar (no kid-ding).

It's been a long session: six workout rounds and three sparring rounds. That's a lot. I'm drenched, beat, humbled and disgusted with

> Looking at his hands is self-defeating (which one is he going to hit me with next)!

myself for yelling. If nothing else, I'll remember and learn. The dark before the light and all that.

BOXING IN A PHONE BOOTH

1-20-98: Lesson #44

After the usual bag work, we go a round or two with Al wearing the glove on his left and the mitt on his right. My moves are much improved today. Head, hands and feet are a little more active and a tad more decisive. I slip some and land some. Problem: shooting punches with my eyes down. It's a very bad habit. I must force myself to keep my eyes on my target. The nano second I duck and lose sight of him is totally confusing and frightening. It's a nerve thing. You gotta go in there and face the music. It ain't gonna feel any better getting hit blind. Putting your head in a hole like that is suicide.

Next, something different. Al has me "box in a telephone booth." He corrals me in a little cul-de-sac made with the punching pillars and has me trade punches with him face to face. It's fast and furious. I'm throwing jabs, rights and hooks — Boom, Boom, Boom — nonstop, while he's throwing with punch mitts (this time on both hands). It's absolutely exhausting and I actually give up at one point — hey, I'm tired. Al says *30 more seconds, come on!* and I slop through. I rest a second and ask to go one more round. I feel I have to redeem myself. It goes much better.

Despite my fatigue, I appreciate what the drill does in terms of simulating real in-fighting. Since you're not getting hit with gloves (only the mitts), you can go until you drop and get a feel for the blazing give-and-take of a real bout.

SPARRING WITH THE KIDS
1-22-98: Lesson #45

Al calls a special sparring session for his boxing students. Three average looking high-school guys show up. No hulking brutes. No intimidation. I *was* a little anxious, but after looking at them, it doesn't look like a big deal.

I start things off with one of the guys (Jordan) and it goes OK. Relaxed. Just working on the jab for a three-minute round. I feel confident and score pretty much when I want to. We don't hit hard. Maybe half speed. I stay in for another guy (John) who is a little more intense (his wandering feet make loud squeaking noises) but I keep it cool as before. I take some shots because I'm a bit too mellow and don't move enough. I hit him here and there and could have done more, but I feel it's better just to keep things serene.

I sit one out and watch John try to dismantle the next fellow (Ryan). Jordan and I look at each other and I say *I don't think we were throwing like that.* He agrees. Poor Ryan sorta covers up and takes it. He's a bit pigeon-toed and with his lanky posture looks totally out of his element. Al keeps a close watch on everything, however, and makes sure it doesn't get out of hand.

We go back to it with license to use both hands and my pace is about the same as before. With Jordan, it's again an evenly paced give-and-take. With John there are again moments of flurry, and I'm a little concerned about the emotion of the bout — I don't want either of us to get serious. He scores and I score. He tries to hit harder but I think it's mostly the excitement. In working his body, I hit below the belt a couple of times. I ask if he's OK and he says yeah.

John and Ryan bout again, and Ryan shows improvement. He moves better, doesn't shell up and throws a few. By this time the guys are getting tired, and I'm surprised to find that I'm probably in better shape than they are. But then I have been doing this since July. The others are relatively new at it.

In another room I go one round with Al, working on slips and jabs. With Al I need to move. It's the only way I can successfully defend myself and get a punch or two in. It goes much better than the last time I sparred with him. Heck, I even land a jab or two.

Working with the students boosted my ego because I felt I pretty much dictated the action. With Al it's a whole new ball game. I have little confidence in my ability to spar with him because our skill levels are so far apart. Alan's slips are awesome. His reflexes are very fast. I try to keep my eyes on his chest or face and off his hands.

> **An. awesome looking Alonzo Highsmith demolishes some fat slob with three or four powerful jabs.**

This helps. Looking at his hands is self defeating (which one is he going to hit me with next?)!

I'm very happy with my sparring performance today. Alotta fun.

Looking at the video the next day:
I gotta move more! Man, I'm lumbering out there. Way too relaxed. I must work my rhythm and sharpen my punches. I guess I was so concerned about hitting someone that I just went through the motions. Not too bad, but even if I decide to lay back, I should still show some spunk on defense -- especially with my slips. Also dropped my guard whenever I went to the body. Al freezes the action at one point and my right hand is practically dragging the floor. And a couple of those low blows I gave John were *really* low. Glad I wasn't throwing hard.

The night before at the fights:
Al and I go to the Sports Arena to watch the Super Bowl Week Fights. There's a lightweight fight that showcases some OK boxing, a welterweight fight that's not so hot, a women's exhibition that is marginally entertaining (light on skills) and a heavyweight match featuring the grandson of Jack Dempsey. Josh Dempsey confidently KOs a more muscular guy who looks like he could take on a lion (looks are deceiving!).

In the feature bout an awesome looking Alonzo Highsmith (former NFL star running back with a bad knee) demolishes some fat slob with three or four powerful jabs (Highsmith never uses his right). This is a laughable mismatch. The loser had D cups!

For Al and I it's a classroom. The crowd is loud and raucous while we quietly study technique. I'm impressed with the speed and movement of the lightweight fighters in particular. I know I'm way too slow with my actions and watching these guys buzz about is truly inspiring.

ONLY LOOKS SIMPLE 1-29-98: Lesson #47

Bag work. I think it's losing its glamour. And why is it that punching the pillar is less satisfying than working my hanging bag at home? Just doesn't have the crisp pop and response. The pillar is starting to leak (it's water filled). Al seems to think that I'm beating it to death (finally, after six months!).

After the bag routine, Al has me work on two responses to a jab. One is a quick overhand right thrown over the opponent's jab and the other is a slip and a jab. The first is more or less a reaction punch that can be successful because the right extends farther than your opponent's jab. Even if you miss with it, it'll block the incoming jab and put your opponent on notice that his jab may elicit your right hand.

The slip and jab are not new, but there are some nuances we go over. The jab is thrown with a slip that is a rather precise dipping of the left shoulder. My tendency is to lean back or sway with the slip, which takes me away from the punch. The right way to do it entails a small movement of the head and shoulders — just enough to make your opponent's punch miss.

I work on the above with Al and his punch mitts, then on the pillar by myself. With the mitts it feels good. On the pillar I feel a little awkward. Slips are elusive to master and only look simple (like alotta this boxing stuff). It's a unique and valuable skill. I wanna get it down.

Guess it's a hard session today. I'm soaked.

WHAT I STILL DON'T KNOW 2-3-98: Lesson #48

Boxing is difficult. Have I said that?

A sparring lesson with Al today is exhausting and frustrating. Haven't I learned anything? Am I in such miserable shape? After the usual bag work we go three rounds or so. I hit his gloves, he hits me. I'm sloppy. No form. No snap. And tired, tired, tired.

The worst thing: I lose eye contact a coupla times as I duck his punches and do this spinning thing to get outta there. This is a freaky reflex response and totally without fundamental merit as I'm

> It's some-thing new – ballroom boxing. The boxing comes in handy when your partner steps on your toe.

turning my back to my opponent – the worst kind of mistake. I have to keep my eyes on the target!

Something gained: I did learn how to wrestle my way out of a corner. Duck inside, grasp an elbow and spin out. This is helpful because I'm always getting backed into the wall and at a loss what to do.

Addressing my hang-dog, Al says it's unrealistic to jump into a sparring situation and think I can apply everything I've been working on. It all goes out the window in the heat of a bout. You can only work on one or two things at the most. He says I might wanna work on slips and jabs, say. Defensive stuff with just enough offense to keep the guy honest. Yeah, oh well ... but absolutely rock-solid advice ... as usual.

What was genuinely amusing today was our sharing the room with a ballroom dancing instructor and her student. Before class, this attractive lady comes up to me and asks if she can share the space. I say sure but that I make alotta noise with the bag. She says they won't even hear it ... and they don't. Although I'm banging away, grunting and cursing my miserable performance throughout the hour, the two ladies (her student is a women) are concentrating so hard on their steps that they hardly notice the boxing lesson or the sparring.

They've got this Guy Lombardo music playing and it's a hoot throwing leather along with it. It's so incongruous. Like something out of an old Monty Python movie. Here's this gracious dancing alongside my bashing and bumbling. Must have been pretty funny to watch.

At one point three little old ladies come in and marvel at the two different lessons in progress. I say it's something new – ballroom boxing. The boxing comes in handy when your partner steps on your toe. This remark brings down the house. *Ballroom boxing! Well, I never!*

THE DAY I LAND MY RIGHT 2-5-98: Lesson #49

Much improved session today. I eat a little something before I show up (I usually eat nothing before noon). It seems to help my energy level a bit. We do this exercise with the punch mitts where I roll off punches and counter from the weighted side. Al throws a punch, I block and roll in the direction it takes and throw from that side since my weight has transferred there. We practice different punches in various combinations and as we pick it up it gets pretty exciting. Another instructor has an older fellow in the room with us today and they're mesmerized with the back-and-forth whacking that's going on. Maybe they think it's real. I do very well at first, but toward the end I start forgetting my responses. It could be fatigue. It's something that's happened before — strong start, wobbly finish.

We spar for about three rounds and it goes so much better than Tuesday. I concentrate on keeping my eyes on Al's face and catch myself twice before I duck and spin. Everything improves if you keep your opponent in sight! I slip OK and actually land a jab or two. In the last round I hit Al on the jaw with a right. And that is a first!

MAD MAN 2-12-98: Sparring Session #2

Sparring is almost full on. We all go at it at least 80%. I'm very happy with my performance. Mixed it up, landed a few, moved pretty good. Got mad at John, the surly teen with the squeaky sneakers. He belts me a time or two and I wallop him (I actually say this after he slugs me: *You go full speed like that again and so will I. And you won't it.*) Al stops things, of course, before they get serious. John's mad because he has a harder time hitting me today (and I score a lot), and I'm mad because he doesn't let up on his punches. I try to make amends (a little), but he's not really into being friends, so there it is. Later, Al tells me that he's a kid and I can't expect him to pull his punches like I can.

Jordan is a well mannered, talkative fellow whose older brother boxes. He has more of a boxer's style than the other two. It's less slugging and more tagging with this guy (which is fine).

> ## To be honest it felt good popping the guy.

Ryan is a straight ahead fighter. Even more so than John. He's tall with a reach that forces me to time his punches to get inside and score. I bang him on the forehead with a right that he later says made him dizzy. He's a nice guy and wears braces. I'm concerned about hitting him in the mouth.

I fight jabbing and full on rounds with John, a jabbing round with Jordan and a full on round with Ryan. It's interesting to see how we develop with each other. It sure is fun and despite the flare-up with John I think we all enjoy our little battles. Al is superb as a coach, knowing when to let us go and when to reign us in. He's got a real feel for this stuff.

Al gives us all a review afterward. He's glowing with my performance but mentions that I shouldn't get mad. Later that night I start to feel bad about losing it (like I always do). I think I shouldn't get upset because I'm older and all that. Although to be honest it felt good popping the guy.

Reviewing Sparring Session #2

We look at the video of last Thursday's sparring. It's a riot watching me growl at John about his full-speed punches (and a little embarrassing, too). I watch myself try to bully him around, even pushing and shoving. It's obvious the kid didn't know what the problem was and I look foolish. Al thinks it's hilarious and goes over the incidents a few times for laughs. I guess it is pretty amusing. I say the kid must hate me, but Al says not at all. Kids forget stuff right away. Not to worry.

I watch myself whale on Ryan and stop him with a hard right. We go over that shot, too. We agree that it's the best punch I've ever thrown. Set it up with a left and POW!

My best work was during the first two jab-only rounds. I was fresh and moving around really well. I slipped a lot of punches and landed a ton of jabs. I think I looked good. Much better than the first time. We all looked better.

SPARRING WITH AL 3-12-98: Lesson #57

After a lukewarm bag session, Alan and I spar for the first time in weeks. We go three rounds doing jabs only and it feels pretty good. Moving my head well. Al hits me a couple of times but misses a lot too. He's impressed. I'm a little rusty during the first round and throw two blind punches, but that's the worst of it. Of course, I don't score much, but I do tag his midsection a few times. The positive is my gaining composure after a wobbly start and boxing with some poise. I feel confident, less intimidated. This probably from moving well *(I can't hit you but you can't hit me either!)*. A very good session and fun. I think I need to spar more. The learning is fast and hard. I think I'm ready for it.

Bag work is important but I'd rather do most of that as homework. Maybe go over new things and work it out on my own. New stuff includes combining blocks, slips and ducks with the standard fare of punches. I'm lousy at it. I need to develop imagination. I throw a jab, my imaginary opponent slips and counters with a right, I block and roll, counter with a right and a hook, etc. I find myself slopping through the motions when Al tells me to do all this. I guess I'm fighting the concept a little. Like it's too boring or something. But I know I must overcome it because that's how it's done when you're on your own.

Are you barbarians finished?

After class, two older ladies come in and ask if we "barbarians" are finished. We laugh (they're just fooling around) and say sure. One of them asks what we'd do if one of us decked the other. I say I've been there and I would shake it off. No problem (right!). Al says he'd just smile, which could very well be true, but then what are the chances of me decking Al in the near future (or ever)? However, I do point out that Al is soaked (true) from the effort of going three rounds with me which indicates the seriousness he takes our bouts.

HERO 3-24-98: Lesson #60:

We go over footwork technique on the pillar and with the mitts, but the real news today concerns one of my young sparring partners, Ryan. Alan tells me that he got into a fight at school. A bully picked a fight with him in front of half the student body and Ryan *kicked*

> ## It's a classic. The gawky kid stands up to his tormentor and knocks his block off.

his butt. The troublemaker had no idea. He thought he'd have an easy go with the lanky, kinda clumsy-looking kid and got the old one-two instead.

Apparently it went something like this:

The bully went up to Ryan and claimed that he'd bad-mouthed him. This wasn't true, of course, and was only a ploy to egg Ryan on. Ryan said he hadn't but suggested that they settle it for good because this kind of badgering had happened before. Bully-boy said OK and to his surprise Ryan went into his boxer's stance. Ryan immediately delivered a number of jabs and knocked the kid down with a right. The bully got up, wrestled Ryan down and kicked his head. But Ryan got up and smacked the perpetrator around as before until they were pulled apart. The overwhelming consensus was that it was Ryan's victory all the way. Even the bully's friends said so.

Al beams as he tells the story and I'm absolutely delighted. It's a classic. The gawky kid stands up to his tormentor and knocks his block off — triumphantly facing irrational aggression as well as his own fears.

Just like the movies. Only better because it really happened. This is a watershed in a young man's life. A moment in time when he discovers his own power and courage. And how appropriate that he used boxing skills. No bat. No gun. No lawsuit. He built his victory with a series of clean left jabs followed by a strong right. Ryan met the challenge of one bad egg and probably eliminated the physical threat posed by all the others. He will never be taken lightly again.

We're sparring again in a week or so and I'm looking forward to congratulating him on his first victory *outside* the ring. Yeah Ryan.

Glossary of Terms

Arm Punch: A punch thrown from the shoulder only, without help from the legs or torso.

Bag Gloves: Boxing gloves designed to hit punching bags. Usually have a flat striking surface.

Champ: Refers to the Heavyweight Champion of the World.
Corralling: A sweeping punching technique used to contain a foot-loose opponent.
Counterpunching: Punching into the exposed or unguarded area an opponent leaves as he punches.

Duck: Moving under a punch by bending at the knees and coming back up in the direction of the punch in a **V** motion.

Heavy Bag: A large punching bag either suspended from above or attached to a heavy foundation.

Inside Fighting: Boxing within the striking zone. Usually entails furious offensive action with short punches and side-to-side head motion. Also in-fighting.

Jab: Punch thrown with the leading hand. This is a straight shot from the chin powered by the arm and sometimes the hips. The busiest punch in boxing.

KO: Knock out.

Left Hook: A power punch thrown with a hooked left arm powered by leg and torso.
Long Rhythm: An easy back and forth motion between the feet.

One-Two: The jab and straight right combination.
One-Two-Three: The jab, straight right and left hook combination.
Outside Fighting: Boxing outside the striking zone. Usually entails active footwork and jabs. Also range fighting.

Parries: Arm and hand movements executed to redirect incoming punches.
Power Punch: Any punch powered by legs and torso.

Punch Mitts: Pads that slip over the hands used to catch punches during training drills.

Queensbury Rules: The prizefighting rules developed by the Marquess of Queensbury in 1866 that stipulated gloves, three-minute rounds and a ban on wrestling.

Reaction Punches: Punches thrown in immediate reaction to an opponent's punch and into the exposed or unguarded area an opponent leaves as he punches.
Right-Left: The straight right and left hook combination.
Round: The two- or three-minute periods that make up a bout.

Shadowboxing: A training exercise where a boxer practices and perfects technique on his own, usually in front of a mirror.
Short Rhythm: The busy side-to-side head motion that accompanies inside fighting or in-fighting.
Slips: Slight movements of the head and neck to avoid punches.
Sparring: Practice boxing. Closely supervised training bouts between fighters often designed to develop specific areas of technical proficiency.
Sparring Gloves: Specially designed and padded boxing gloves used for sparring.
Squaring Off: Coming out of the sideways boxer's stance and facing an opponent with an open chest.
Straight Right: A power punch thrown with a straight hand powered by leg and torso.

Underhand Jab: A sweeping upward punch thrown with the leading hand from the waist.
Uppercut: A power punch thrown up from the waist powered by legs and torso.

Wraps: The long strips of cloth used to wrap and protect the hands before putting on boxing gloves.

Resources

Where to Learn
Check out the yellow pages under boxing for the gym nearest you. If nothing else, you'll get a salty dose of reality. However, the sport also lurks in malls and uptown fitness centers these days, so give them a try, too. For further help and recommendations call USA Boxing: 719-578-4506.

General Information:
Library
Your local library will probably have more than a few boxing books and videos.
in boxing.

Equipment
Your local sporting goods store or outlet will have stuff, but I suggest you buy directly from one of the top manufacturers.

Everlast:	718-993-0100
Ringside:	913-888-1719
Title Boxing:	913-831-1122

Magazines
The Boxing Record Book
Fight Fax, Inc.
PO Box 896
Sicklerville, NJ 08081-0896
609-782-8868

Boxing USA
United States Amateur Boxing, Inc. (USA Boxing)
One Olympic Plaza
Colorado Springs, CO 80909
719-578-4506

Boxing (year)
KO Magazine
Ring
Ring Boxing Almanac and Book of Facts
Ring Extra
Ring Presents
World Boxing

(All the above)
London Publishing Company
7002 West Butler Pike
Ambler, PA 19002-5147
215-643-6385

Hispanics in Boxing
R. Paniagua, Incorporated
155 East 42nd Street
Suite 206
New York, NY 10017-5618
212-983-4444

International Boxing Digest (Boxing Illustrated)
International Sports Ltd.
530 Fifth Avenue
Suite 430
New York, NY 10036
212-730-1374

Ring Rhetoric
American Association for the Improvement of Boxing
86 Fletcher Avenue
Mount Vernon, NY 10552-3319
914-664-4571

Movies

That Hollywood has had a strong interest in boxing over the years shouldn't be surprising. The sport brings it all to the table: violent conflict, courage, redemption, individual struggle, good guys, bad guys ... the whole enchilada. Since 1922 over 130 films have been made about boxing. Here's a small, yet sparkling, sampling that spans six decades. Note that they feature some of Hollywood's greatest stars over the years.

Gentleman Jim (1942)
Errol Flynn
Body and Soul (1947)
John Garfield
Champion (1949)
Kirk Douglas
The Set-Up (1949)
Robert Ryan
Somebody Up There Likes Me (1956) Paul Newman
Requiem for a Heavyweight (1962) Anthony Quinn
Rocky (1976)
Sylvester Stallone
Raging Bull (1980)
Robert DeNiro
The Boxer (1998)
Daniel Day-Lewis

Museums

International Boxing
Hall of Fame
Hall of Fame Drive
PO Box 425
Canastota, NY 13032

315-697-7095
Fax 315-697-5356

Organizations:
Amateur

Golden Gloves
Association
of America
1503 Linda Lane
Hutchinson, KS 67502
615-522-5885
Fax 615-544-3829

International Amateur
Boxing Association
135 Westervelt Place
Creskill, NJ 07626
201-567-3117

Knights Boxing
Team International
2350 Ventura Road
Smyrna, GA 30080-1327
770-432-3632
Fax 770-528-2132

United States Amateur
Boxing, Inc. (USA Boxing)
One Olympic Plaza
Colorado Springs, CO 80909
719-578-4506
Fax: 719-632-3426
E-mail: usaboxing@aol.com

Professional

International Boxing
Federation (IBF)
134 Evergreen Place, 9th Floor
East Orange, NJ 07018
201-414-0300

North American
Boxing Federation
14340 Sundance Drive
Reno, NV 89511
702-853-1236
Fax 702-853-1724

World Boxing
Association (WBA)
www.wbaonline.com

World Boxing Council (WBC)
Genova 33, Oficina 503
Colonia Juarez
Cuauhtemoc
06600 Mexico City, DF, Mexico

World Boxing
Organization (WBO)
412 Colorado Avenue
Aurora, IL 60506
630-897-4765
Fax 630-897-1134

Other Boxing Organizations
American Association
for the Improvement of Boxing
36 Fletcher Avenue
Mount Vernon, NY 10552
914-664-4571

International Boxing
Writers Association
50 Mary Street
Tappan, NY 10983
914-359-6334

International Veteran
Boxers Association
35 Brady Avenue
New Rochelle, NY 10805

914-235-6820
Fax 914-654-9785

Television
There's lots of boxing on the
tube. Check your listings. By the
way, when television first began,
boxing was one of its biggest
draws. Boxing could be seen
every night of the week during
the 1950s and its ratings rivaled
those of *I Love Lucy.*

These are the networks and programs that provide the action as
this book goes to print:

ESPN
ESPN2
Fox Sport Network
HBO's Boxing After Dark
Pay-Per-View
Showtime Feature Events
USA's Tuesday Night Fights

Videos:
Blockbuster
Look in the sports or special
interest sections. You may be surprised. In my local outlet I found
six hard-core boxing videos
including tapes on Julio Caesar
Chavez, Mike Tyson, Muhammad
Ali and Sugar Ray Robinson.

Ringside
They have all the boxing videos
known to man. Check out their
catalog: 913-888-1719.

Bibliography

Brooke-Ball, Peter. *The Boxing Album*. New York, New York. : Smithmark Publishers Inc., 1992.

Brown, John. *Boxing Manual*. Lenexa, Kansas.: Ringside, Inc., 1996.

DePasquale, Peter. *The Boxer's Workout*. Brooklyn, New York.: Fighting Fit Inc., 1988.

Grombach, V. John. *The Saga of Sock*. New York, New York.: A. S. Barns and Company, 1949.

Ringside Products. *Ringside Training Video*. Lenexa, Kansas.: Ringside, Inc., 1996.

Sammons, T. Jeffrey. *Beyond the Ring: The Role of Boxing in American Society*. Chicago, Illinois.: University of Illinois Press, 1988.

USA Boxing. *Coaching Olympic Style Boxing*. Carmel, Indiana.: Cooper Publishing Group LLC, 1995.

Ward, Douglas. *Ringside Report*. Lenexa, Kansas.: Ringside, Inc.

Index

About the Author & Start-Up Sports

Doug Werner is the author of all eight books in the *Start-Up Sports Series* including *Surfer's, Snowboarder's, Sailor's, In-Line Skater's, Bowler's, Longboarder's, Golfer's* and *Fencer's Start-Up*. He has been interviewed on CNN and numerous radio talk shows throughout the United States. His books have appeared on ESPN, been featured in prominent national publications, and sold throughout the United States, Canada, Great Britain and Japan.

Doug Werner

The series celebrates the challenge of learning a new sport with emphasis on basic technique, safety and fun. Imbued with a unique beginner's perspective, *Start-Up* books explain and explore what it's really like to learn.

Each book has the endorsement of prominent individuals, publications and organizations in each respective sport including Steve Hawk of *Surfer Magazine*, Ted Martin of International Snowboard Federation, Chuck Nichols of America's Cup 1995, National In-Line Hockey Association, *Bowler's Journal, Longboarder Magazine, Ski Magazine, Snow Country, Veteran Fencer's Quarterly* and many others.

The series has received critical acclaim from *Booklist, Library Journal, Outside Kids, Boys Life, The San Francisco Examiner* and *The Orange County Register.*

Werner is a graduate of Cal State Long Beach and holds a degree in fine arts. In previous lifetimes he established a graphics business in 1980, an advertising agency in 1984 and yet another graphics business in 1987. By 1993 he had decided to move on and began writing sport instructional guides. In 1994 he established Tracks Publishing and the *Start-Up Sports* series. Doug has pursued a sporting lifestyle his entire life and has resided in San Diego, California, one of the planet's major sport funzones, since 1980.

About the Coach

Alan Lachica

Alan is a certified USA Amateur Boxing coach, the former owner and operator of Cross Boxing in San Diego and a former amateur boxer — winning over 90% of his competitive bouts. His boxing exhibitions have been featured on local and national television broadcasts including *Eye on America* (CBS News).

Lachica is also a certified personal trainer. His clients have included top professional athletes in Major League Baseball and the National Football League.

He is a graduate of Cal State Long Beach and currently lives in La Jolla, California.

For further information about his boxing and training programs call 619-804-6688.

Ordering More Start-UpSports **Books**

The *Start-Up Sports* series includes guides on surfing, snowboarding, sailing, in-line skating, roller hockey, bowling, longboard surfing, golfing, fencing and boxing.

Each book costs $12.95 that includes priority postage.
Send a check for this amount to:

Tracks Publishing 140 Brightwood Ave. Chula Vista, CA 91910

Or call 1-800-443-3570. Visa and MasterCard accepted.

(**www.startupsports.com**)